FAST TALK

Italian

I0979766

lonely planet

Fast Talk Italian
1st edition – May 2004

Published by
Lonely Planet Publications Pty Ltd ABN 36 005 607 983
90 Maribyrnong St, Footscray, Victoria 3011, Australia

Lonely Planet Offices
Australia Locked Bag 1, Footscray, Victoria 3011
USA 150 Linden St, Oakland CA 94607
UK 72-82 Rosebery Ave, London, EC1R 4RW

Publisher Roz Hopkins
Publishing Manager Peter D'Onghia
Commissioning Editors Karin Vidstrup Monk, Karina Coates
Project Manager Fabrice Rocher
Series Designer Yukiyoshi Kamimura
Layout Designer Patrick Marris
Editors Piers Kelly, Annelies Mertens
Also thanks to Karina Coates, Pietro Iagnocco and Mirna Cicione

Photography
Little baby Fiat by Jonathan Smith
© Lonely Planet Images 2004

ISBN 1 74059 995 0

text © Lonely Planet Publications Pty Ltd 2004

10 9 8 7 6   4 3 2 1

Printed by the Bookmaker International Ltd
Printed in China

CHAT 6

EXPLORE 13

SHOP 20

ENJOY 26

EAT & DRINK 28

CONTENTS

3

CONTENTS

Language name: Italian

Italian is known to its native speakers as *italiano* ee·tal·*ya*·no

Language family: Romance

Italian belongs to the Romance family of languages and is a close relative of Spanish, French, Portuguese and Romanian.

Key country & secondary countries:

The key country where Italian is spoken is of course Italy, but Italian is also spoken by minorities in Switzerland, Slovenia, France and the Istrian peninsula of Croatia where the language has official status.

Approximate number of speakers:

Nearly 65 million people speak Italian worldwide. Many of those who live in Italy also speak a dialect specific to their native region.

Donations to English:

English speakers will recognise many Italian words related to music, cuisine and art. Opera, virtuoso, broccoli, spaghetti and fresco are just a few.

Grammar:

The structure of Italian holds no major surprises for English speakers due to the common Latin ancestry of the two languages.

Pronunciation:

With the exception of the rolled *r*, the sounds of Italian can almost all be found in English. You'll be surprised how easy it is to pronounce Italian words.

Abbreviations used in this book:

| m | masculine | sg | singular | pol | polite |
| f | feminine | pl | plural | inf | informal |

CHAT
Meeting & greeting

Hello.	*Buongiorno/Salve.* pol	bwon·*jor*·no/*sal*·ve
Hi.	*Ciao.* inf	chow
Good morning/ afternoon.	*Buongiorno.*	bwon·*jor*·no
Good evening.	*Buonasera.*	bwo·na·*se*·ra
Good night.	*Buonanotte.*	bwo·na·*no*·te
Goodbye.	*Arrivederci.* pol	a·ree·ve·*der*·chee
Bye.	*Ciao.* inf	chow
Mr/Sir	*Signore*	see·*nyo*·re
Mrs/Madam	*Signora*	see·*nyo*·ra
Miss/Ms	*Signorina*	see·nyo·*ree*·na
Doctor	*Dottore/Dottoressa* m/f	do·*to*·re/do·to·*re*·sa

Essentials

Yes.	*Sì.*	see
No.	*No.*	no
Please.	*Per favore.*	per fa·*vo*·re
Thank you (very much).	*Grazie (mille).*	*gra*·tsye (*mee*·le)
You're welcome.	*Prego.*	*pre*·go
Excuse me.	*Mi scusi.* pol	mee *skoo*·zee
	Scusami. inf	*skoo*·za·mee
Sorry.	*Mi dispiace.*	mee dees·*pya*·che

How are you?
  Come sta? pol   ko·me sta
  Come stai? inf   ko·me stai

Fine. And you?
  Bene. E Lei/tu? pol/inf   be·ne e lay/too

What's your name?
  Come si chiama? pol   ko·me see kya·ma
  Come ti chiami? inf   ko·me tee kya·mee

My name is ...
  Mi chiamo ...   mee kya·mo ...

I'd like to introduce you to ...
  Le/Ti presento ... pol/inf   le/tee pre·zen·to ...

I'm pleased to meet you.
  Piacere.   pya·che·re

It's been great meeting you.
  È stato veramente un   e sta·to ve·ra·men·te oon
  piacere conoscerla/   pya·che·re ko·no·sher·la/
  conoscerti. pol/inf   ko·no·sher·tee

This is my ...	*Le/Ti presento ...* pol/inf	le/tee pre·zen·to ...
colleague	*il mio collega* m	eel mee·o ko·le·ga
	la mia collega f	la mee·a ko·le·ga
friend	*il mio amico* m	eel mee·o a·mee·ko
	la mia amica f	la mee·a a·mee·ka
husband	*mio marito*	mee·o ma·ree·to
partner	*il mio*	eel mee·o
(intimate)	*compagno* m	kom·pa·nyo
	la mia	la mee·a
	compagna f	kom·pa·nya
wife	*mia moglie*	mee·a mo·lye

7

I'm here ...	*Sono qui ...*	*so*·no kwee ...
for a holiday	*in vacanza*	een va·*kan*·tsa
on business	*per affari*	per a·*fa*·ree
to study	*per motivi*	per mo·*tee*·vee
	di studio	dee *stoo*·dyo
with my family	*con la mia*	kon la *mee*·a
	famiglia	fa·*mee*·lya
with my partner	*con il mio*	kon eel *mee*·o
	compagno m	kom·*pa*·nyo
	con la mia	kon la *mee*·a
	compagna f	kom·*pa*·nya

How long are you here for?

| *Quanto tempo si fermerà?* pol | kwan·to *tem*·po see fer·me·*ra* |
| *Quanto tempo ti fermerai?* inf | kwan·to *tem*·po tee fer·me·*rai* |

I'm here for ... days/weeks.

| *Sono qui per ... giorni/* | *so*·no kwee per ... *jor*·nee/ |
| *settimane.* | se·tee·*ma*·ne |

For numbers see the box feature in **LOOK UP**, page 67.

Here's my ...	*Ecco il mio ...*	e·ko eel *mee*·o ...
What's your ...?	*Qual'è il Suo/*	kwa·*le* eel *soo*·o/
	tuo ...?	*too*·o ...
address	*indirizzo*	een·dee·*ree*·tso
email address	*indirizzo di*	een·dee·*ree*·tso dee
	email	e·mayl
fax number	*numero di fax*	*noo*·me·ro dee faks
home number	*numero di casa*	*noo*·me·ro dee *ka*·za
mobile number	*numero di*	*noo*·me·ro dee
	cellulare	che·loo·*la*·re
work number	*numero di*	*noo*·me·ro dee
	lavoro	la·*vo*·ro

Breaking the language barrier

Do you speak English?
Parla inglese?   *par·la een·gle·ze*

Does anyone speak English?
C'è qualcuno che parla inglese?   *che kwal·koo·no ke par·la een·gle·ze*

Do you understand?
Capisce?   *ka·pee·she*

I understand.
Capisco.   *ka·pee·sko*

I don't understand.
Non capisco.   *non ka·pee·sko*

I speak a little.
Parlo un po'.   *par·lo oon po*

What does 'vietato' mean?
Che cosa vuol dire 'vietato'?   *ke ko·za vwol dee·re vye·ta·to*

How do you ...?	*Come si ...?*	*ko·me see ...*
pronounce this	*pronuncia questo*	*pro·noon·cha kwe·sto*
write 'arrivederci'	*scrive 'arrivederci'*	*skree·ve a·ree·ve·der·chee*

Could you please ...?	*Può ... per favore?*	*pwo ... per fa·vo·re*
repeat that	*ripeterlo*	*ree·pe·ter·lo*
speak more slowly	*parlare più lentamente*	*par·la·re pyoo len·ta·men·te*
write it down	*scriverlo*	*skree·ver·lo*

9

Personal details

Where are you from?
Da dove viene/vieni? pol/inf   da *do*·ve vye·ne/vye·nee

I'm from ...	Vengo ...	ven·go ...
England	dall'Inghilterra	da·leen·geel·te·ra
New Zealand	dalla Nuova	da·la nwo·va
	Zelanda	ze·lan·da
the USA	dagli Stati	da·lyee sta·tee
	Uniti	oo·nee·tee

I'm ...	Sono ...	so·no ...
married	sposato/a m/f	spo·za·to/a
separated	separato/a m/f	se·pa·ra·to/a
single (man)	celibe	che·lee·be
single (woman)	nubile	noo·bee·le

Occupations & study

What's your occupation?
Che lavoro fa/fai? pol/inf   ke la·vo·ro fa/fai

I'm a/an ...	Sono ...	so·no ...
manual worker	manovale m&f	ma·no·va·le
office worker	impiegato/a m/f	eem·pye·ga·to/a
tradesperson	operaio/a m/f	o·pe·ra·yo/a

I'm ...	Sono ...	so·no ...
retired	pensionato/a m/f	pen·syo·na·to/a
unemployed	disoccupato/a m/f	dee·zo·koo·pa·to/a

I work in ...	*Lavoro nel campo ...*	la·*vo*·ro nel *kam*·po ...
administration	*dell'amministrazione*	de·la·mee·nee·stra·*tsyo*·ne
public relations	*delle relazioni pubbliche*	*de*·le re·la·*tsyo*·nee *poo*·blee·ke
retail	*della vendità al minuto*	*de*·la ven·dee·*ta* al mee·*noo*·to

I'm studying ...	*Sto studiando ...*	sto stoo·*dyan*·do ...
arts/humanities	*lettere*	*le*·te·re
business	*commercio*	ko·*mer*·cho
engineering	*ingegneria*	een·je·nye·*ree*·a

Age

How old ...?	*Quanti anni ...?*	*kwan*·tee *a*·nee ...
are you	*ha/hai* pol/inf	a/ai
is your son	*ha Suo figlio*	a *soo*·o *fee*·lyo
is your daughter	*ha Sua figlia*	a *soo*·a *fee*·lya

I'm ... years old.
Ho ... anni. o ... *a*·nee

For your age, see the box feature in **LOOK UP**, page 67.

Feelings

I'm ...	*Ho ...*	o ...
I'm not ...	*Non ho ...*	non o ...
Are you ...?	*Ha/Hai ...?* pol/inf	a/ai ...
cold	*freddo*	*fre*·do
hungry	*fame*	*fa*·me
sleepy	*sonno*	*so*·no

I'm ...	Sono ...	so·no ...
I'm not ...	Non sono ...	non so·no ...
Are you ...?	È/Sei ...? pol/inf	e/say ...
embarrassed	imbarazzato/a m/f	eem·ba·ra·tsa·to/a
happy	felice	fe·lee·che
worried	preoccupato/a m/f	pre·o·koo·pa·to/a

Beliefs

I'm ...	Sono ...	so·no ...
I'm not ...	Non sono ...	non so·no ...
atheist	ateo/a m/f	a·te·o/a
Buddhist	buddista	boo·dee·sta
Catholic	cattolico/a m/f	ka·to·lee·ko/a
Christian	cristiano/a m/f	krees·tya·no/a
Hindu	indù	een·doo
Jewish	ebreo/a m/f	e·bre·o/a
Muslim	musulmano/a m/f	moo·sool·ma·no/a
religious	religioso/a m/f	re·lee·jo·zo/a

Weather

What's the weather like?

Che tempo fa?		ke tem·po fa

It's ...	Fa ...	fa ...
cold	freddo	fre·do
(very) hot	(molto) caldo	(mol·to) kal·do
warm	bel tempo	bel tem·po

It's ...		
freezing	Si gela.	see je·la
rainy	Piove.	pyo·ve
windy	Tira vento.	tee·ra ven·to

EXPLORE
Doing the sights

What would you do if you only had one day?
Lei che farebbe se avesse   lay ke fa·*re*·be se a·*ve*·se
solo una giornata?   *so*·lo *oo*·na jor·*na*·ta

Do you have information on local sights?
Avete delle informazioni   a·*ve*·te *de*·le een·for·ma·*tsyo*·nee
su posti locali?   soo *pos*·tee lo·*ka*·lee

I'd like to see …
Vorrei vedere …   vo·*ray* ve·*de*·re …

I have only (one day).
Ho solo (un giorno).   o *so*·lo (oon jor·no)

What sights should I definitely see?
Quali posti dovrei   *kwa*·lee *pos*·tee do·*vray*
assolutamente vedere?   a·so·loo·ta·*men*·te ve·*de*·re

What's that?
Cos'è?   ko·*ze*

Who made it?
Chi l'ha fatto?   kee la *fa*·to

How old is it?
Quanti anni ha?   *kwan*·tee *a*·nee a

I'd like a/an …	*Vorrei …*	vo·*ray* …
audio set	*un auricolare*	oo·now·ree·ko·*la*·re
catalogue	*un catalogo*	oon ka·*ta*·lo·go
guide	*una guida*	*oo*·na *gwee*·da
guidebook in	*una guida*	*oo*·na *gwee*·da
English	*in inglese*	een een·*gle*·ze
local map	*una cartina*	*oo*·na kar·*tee*·na
	della zona	*de*·la *dzo*·na

13

Could you take a photograph of me?
   Può farmi una foto?   pwo far·mee *oo*·na *fo*·to

Can I take a photograph?
   Posso fare una foto?   po·so fa·re *oo*·na *fo*·to

I'll send you the photograph.
   Le spedirò la foto.   le spe·dee·*ro* la *fo*·to

Gallery & museum hopping

When's the ... open?	*A che ora apre ...?*	a ke *o*·ra *a*·pre...
gallery	*la galleria*	la ga·le·*ree*·a
museum	*il museo*	eel moo·*ze*·o

What's in the collection?
   Quali sono le opere   *kwa*·lee *so*·no le *o*·pe·re
   qui esposte?   kwee es·*pos*·te

It's an exhibition of ...
   È una mostra di ...   e *oo*·na *mos*·tra dee ...

I like the works of ...
   Mi piacciono le opere di ...   mee *pya*·cho·no le *o*·pe·re dee ...

It reminds me of ...
   Mi ricorda ...   mee ree·*kor*·da ...

... art	*l'arte ...*	*lar*·te ...
byzantine	*bizantina*	bee·dzan·*tee*·na
futurist	*futurista*	foo·too·*ree*·sta
Gothic	*gotica*	*go*·tee·ka
Renaissance	*rinascimentale*	ree·na·shee·men·*ta*·le
Romanesque	*romanica*	ro·*ma*·nee·ka

Getting in

What's the admission charge?
Quant'è il prezzo kwan·*te* eel *pre*·tso
d'ingresso? deen·*gre*·so

It costs (seven euros).
Costa (sette Euro). *kos*·ta (*se*·te e·*oo*·ro)

What time does it open?
A che ora apre? a ke *o*·ra *a*·pre

What time does it close?
A che ora chiude? a ke *o*·ra kyoo·de

Is there a discount for ...?	*C'è uno sconto per ...?*	che *oo*·no *skon*·to per ...
children	*bambini*	bam·*bee*·nee
families	*famiglie*	fa·*mee*·lye
groups	*gruppi*	*groo*·pee
pensioners	*pensionati*	pen·syo·*na*·tee
students	*studenti*	stoo·*den*·tee

Tours

Can you recommend a ...?	*Può consigliare...?*	pwo kon·see·*lya*·re...
boat trip	*una gita in barca*	*oo*·na *jee*·ta een *bar*·ka
day trip	*un'escursione in giornata*	oo·nes·koor·*syo*·ne een jor·*na*·ta
tour	*una gita turistica*	*oo*·na *jee*·ta too·*ree*·stee·ka

When's the next ...?	*A che ora parte la prossima ...?*	a ke *o*·ra *par*·te la *pro*·see·ma ...
boat trip	*gita in barca*	*jee*·ta een *bar*·ka
day trip	*escursione in giornata*	es·koor·*syo*·ne een jor·*na*·ta
tour	*gita turistica*	*jee*·ta too·ree·*stee*·ka

Is ... included?	*È incluso ...?*	e een·*kloo*·zo ...
accommodation	*l'alloggio*	la·*lo*·jo
the admission charge	*il prezzo d'ingresso*	eel *pre*·tso deen·*gre*·so
food	*il vitto*	eel *vee*·to
transport	*il trasporto*	eel tras·*por*·to

Do I need to take ... with me?
Devo portare ... con me?   de·vo por·*ta*·re ... kon me

The guide will pay.
La guida pagherà.   la *gwee*·da pa·ge·*ra*

The guide has paid.
La guida ha pagato.   la *gwee*·da a pa·*ga*·to

How long is the tour?
Quanto dura la gita?   *kwan*·to *doo*·ra la *jee*·ta

What time should we be back?
A che ora dovremmo ritornare?   a ke *o*·ra dov·*re*·mo ree·tor·*na*·re

I'm with them.
Sono con loro.   *so*·no kon *lo*·ro

I've lost my group.
Ho perso il mio gruppo.   o *per*·so eel *mee*·o *groo*·po

Have you seen a group of (Australians)?
Ha visto un gruppo di (australiani)?   a *vees*·to oon *groo*·po dee (ows·tra·*lya*·nee)

Top 5 day trips

Sometimes the frenzied pace of Italian cities can get a little overwhelming. For a more relaxing alternative, head out of town to enjoy a quieter, off-the-beaten-track cultural experience.

Top day trip excursions from Rome:

Ostia Antica   os·tee·a an·tee·ka
These ruins of Rome's main port for six centuries provide a fascinating insight into a working Roman town. The deserted city was buried in a river of salt so the remains have been wonderfully well preserved.

Tivoli   tee·vo·lee
The hilltop town of Tivoli was once a popular suburban retreat for prominent Romans. Spend the morning touring the sumptuous Villa Adriana, replete with a fishpond, barracks and temples. In the afternoon you can picnic in the stunning gardens of the Villa d'Este, a pleasure palace built in the mid-16th century.

Top day trip excursions from Florence:

Chianti   kyan·tee
Situated in one of the world's most famous wine regions, the surrounding scenery features castles, villages and villas perched picturesquely on hilltops. Don't leave without visiting a winery and tasting some of Chianti's world-famous wine.

Lucca   loo·ka
Lucca is an excellent place to escape the hustle and bustle of Florence. Check out the dazzling Romanesque church of San Michele and admire the strikingly resplendent mosaic in the church of San Frediano.

Siena   sye·na
Set on three hills and flanked by fertile valleys, Siena is a charming city of medieval turrets and towers. Take a stroll around the magnificent 14th-century piazza in the centre of town.

Top 10 sights

From the sultry south to the metropolitan north, Italy flaunts its many centuries of glorious history. It would take a lifetime to explore all the wonders of Italy's fascinating past, but if you don't have that much time on your hands, make sure you pack in a few of these famous highlights:

Pompeii   pom·pay

This world-famous archaeological site near **Naples** is rightly Italy's most popular tourist attraction. Buried after the eruption of Mt Vesuvius in AD 79, the Roman town is still being excavated stone by stone. Spend a day wandering through the Roman streets and let your imagination unfold.

Il Colosseo   eel ko·lo·say·o

Once a venue for gory battles between beasts, slaves and gladiators, the Colosseum has become a symbol of **Rome** itself. In its day it could accommodate a staggering 50,000 spectators.

La Città del Vaticano   la chee·ta del va·tee·ka·no

A must-see for any visitor to **Rome**, the Vatican City is dominated by St Peter's Basilica, a breath-taking structure designed chiefly by Michelangelo. The extensive Vatican museum – boasting magnificent art and curiosities – leads to the Sistine Chapel. Arrive early to beat the crowds.

La Torre Pendente di Pisa   la to·re pen·den·te dee pee·sa

Perhaps the world's most famous architectural disaster, the Leaning Tower of **Pisa** is a sight to behold. The tower is now secure to climb, after a recent 12-year project to prevent it from toppling over completely.

Il Duomo di Firenze   eel dwo·mo dee fee·ren·tse

Built to show off the wealth and supremacy of Tuscany, the *Duomo* sits impressively in the centre of **Florence**, its marvellous terracotta-coloured dome towering above the surrounding buildings. Climb the adjacent bell tower for an unbeatable panoramic view of the city.

EXPLORE

Il Ponte Vecchio   eel *pon*·te *ve*·kyo

Situated in **Florence** on the narrowest point of the river Arno, the *Ponte Vecchio* is a romantic place to visit by day or night. The bridge was once crowded with tanneries and butchers until the 16th century when they were replaced with decorous jewellers that continue to ply their trade here today.

Gli Uffizi   lyee oo·*fee*·tsee

You'll have to get up very early to avoid a long queue for the *Uffizi* in **Florence** but it's well worth the effort. Drift from room to room gazing at Italy's extraordinary artistic legacy. Even those with little knowledge of art will recognise Botticelli's famous *Birth of Venus* and Titian's *Venus of Urbino* – just two of the hundreds of stunning works on display.

La Basilica di San Marco   la ba·*see*·lee·ka dee san *mar*·ko

Towering imposingly over the *Piazza San Marco*, this grand basilica in **Venice** embodies a magnificent blend of decorative styles. The basilica's diverse architectural influences – ranging from Byzantine to Romanesque, Gothic and Renaissance – point to Venice's unique cosmopolitanism, still in evidence today. The inside of the building is adorned with an incredible array of treasures plundered from the East.

Il Duomo di Milano   eel *dwo*·mo dee mee·*la*·no

This massive cathedral is the centrepiece of **Milan**, a Gothic colossus that took over four hundred years to complete. The roof and the facade alone are crammed with 135 spires and 3200 statues.

La Scala   la *ska*·la

The famous opera house of **Milan** with its towering rows of curtained boxes is perhaps one of the most romantic places to experience some of Europe's finest musical talent. If you can't get tickets to the opera at this superb theatre, make sure you visit the enjoined museum which is full of musical oddities such as the plaster cast of Chopin's hands. Admission includes a peep at the theatre's auditorium.

EXPLORE

SHOP
Essentials

Where's ... ?	Dov'è ... ?	do·ve ...
a bank	una banca	oo·na ban·ka
a cake shop	una pasticceria	oo·na pa·stee·che·ree·a
a supermarket	un supermercato	oon soo·per·mer·ka·to

Where can I buy ...?
Dove posso comprare ...?   do·ve po·so kom·pra·re ...

I'd like to buy ...
Vorrei comprare ...   vo·ray kom·pra·re ...

Do you have any others?
Ne avete altri?   ne a·ve·te al·tree

Can I look at it?
Posso dare un'occhiata?   po·so da·re oo·no·kya·ta

I'm just looking.
Sto solo guardando.   sto so·lo gwar·dan·do

Could I have it wrapped, please?
Può incartarlo   pwo een·kar·tar·lo
per favore?   per fa·vo·re

Does it have a guarantee?
Ha la garanzia?   a la ga·ran·tsee·a

Can I have it sent overseas?
Può spedirlo all'estero?   pwo spe·deer·lo a·les·te·ro

Can I pick it up later?
Posso ritirarlo più tardi?   po·so ree·tee·rar·lo pyoo tar·dee

It's faulty/broken.
È difettoso/rotto.   e dee·fe·to·zo/ro·to

20

I'd like . . ., please.	Vorrei . . ., per favore.	vo·ray . . . per fa·vo·re
my change	il mio resto	eel mee·o res·to
my money back	un rimborso	oon reem·bor·so
to change this	cambiare questo	kam·bya·re kwe·sto
to return this	restituire	res·tee·twee·re
	questo	kwe·sto

Hot shop spots

When good shoppers die they go to Italy, a veritable paradise of great spending options. If your wallet is starting to weigh you down, you can quickly lighten it at these renowned shopping locations:

Piazza di Spagna, Rome — major fashion labels • accessories • jewellery • homeware

Via del Governo Vecchio, Rome — second-hand clothes • upcoming Roman designs

Via dei Coronari, Via Margutta, Rome — antiques • art • unusual souvenirs

Medieval Core, Florence — designer clothes • shoes • jewellery

Oltrano, Florence — local crafts • art

San Polo, Venice — carnavale masks • costumes • ceramics • model gondolas

North of Piazza San Marco, Venice — clothing • shoes • accessories

Golden Quad, Milan — expensive designer clothes • accessories • leather shoes • jewellery

SHOP

Paying

How much is it?
Quant'è?
kwan·*te*

Can you write down the price?
Può scrivere il prezzo?
pwo *skree*·ve·re eel *pre*·tso

Can I have smaller notes?
Mi può dare banconote
più piccole?
mee pwo *da*·re ban·ko·*no*·te
pyoo *pee*·ko·le

That's too expensive.
È troppo caro.
e *tro*·po *ka*·ro

Can you lower the price?
Può farmi lo sconto?
pwo *far*·mee lo *skon*·to

Do you have something cheaper?
Ha qualcosa di
meno costoso?
a kwal·*ko*·za dee
me·no kos·*to*·zo

Do you accept ...?	*Accettate ...?*	a·che·*ta*·te ...
credit cards	*la carta di*	la *kar*·ta dee
	credito	*kre*·dee·to
debit cards	*la carta di*	la *kar*·ta dee
	debito	*de*·bee·to
travellers cheques	*gli assegni di*	lyee a·*se*·nyee dee
	viaggio	vee·*a*·jo
I'd like ..., please.	*Vorrei ...,*	vo·*ray* ...
	per favore.	per fa·*vo*·re
a receipt	*una ricevuta*	*oo*·na ree·che·*voo*·ta
my change	*il mio resto*	eel *mee*·o *res*·to
my money back	*un rimborso*	oon reem·*bor*·so

For phrases about banking, see **SERVICES**, page 42.

SHOP

22

Clothes & shoes

I'm looking for …	Sto cercando …	sto cher·*kan*·do …
jeans	*dei jeans*	day jeens
shoes	*delle scarpe*	*de*·le *skar*·pe
underwear	*della biancheria*	*de*·la byan·ke·*ree*·a
	intima	*een*·tee·ma

Can I try it on?
Potrei provarmelo? po·*tray* pro·*var*·me·lo

My size is (42).
Sono una taglia *so*·no *oo*·na *ta*·lya
(quarantadue). (kwa·*ran*·ta·*doo*·e)

It doesn't fit.
Non va bene. non va *be*·ne

small	*piccola*	*pee*·ko·la
medium	*media*	*me*·dya
large	*forte*	*for*·te

It's too …	È troppo …	e *tro*·po
big	*grande*	*gran*·de
small	*piccolo*	*pee*·ko·lo
tight	*stretto*	*stre*·to

Books & music

Is there an English-language bookshop?
C'è una libreria che *oo*·na lee·bre·*ree*·a
specializzata in spe·cha·lee·*dza*·ta een
lingua inglese? *leen*·gwa een·*gle*·ze

Is there an English-language section?
C'è una sezione di che *oo*·na se·*tsyo*·ne dee
lingua inglese? *leen*·gwa een·*gle*·ze

23

Do you have a/an ...   *Avete ...*   a·ve·te
- **book by ...**   *un libro di ...*   oon lee·bro dee ...
- **entertainment guide**   *una guida agli spettacoli*   oo·na gwee·da a·lyee spe·ta·ko·lee

I'd like a ...   *Vorrei ...*   vo·ray ...
- **map (city)**   *una pianta della città*   oo·na pyan·ta de·la chee·ta
- **map (road)**   *una cartina stradale*   oo·na kar·tee·na stra·da·le
- **newspaper (in English)**   *un giornale (in inglese)*   oon jor·na·le (een een·gle·ze)
- **pen**   *una penna*   oo·na pe·na
- **postcard**   *una cartolina*   oo·na kar·to·lee·na

I'd like (a) ...   *Vorrei ...*   vo·ray ...
- **blank tape**   *una cassetta vuota*   oo·na ka·se·ta vwo·ta
- **CD**   *un cidì*   oon chee·dee
- **headphones**   *delle cuffia*   de·le koo·fya

I'm looking for a CD by ...
Sto cercando un cidì di ...   sto cher·kan·do un chee·dee dee ...

I heard a group called ...
Ho sentito un gruppo chiamato ...   o sen·tee·to oon groo·po kya·ma·to ...

What's his/her best recording?
Qual'è la sua migliore incisione?   kwa·le la soo·a mee·lyo·re een·chee·zyo·ne

Can I listen to it here?
Potrei ascoltarlo qui?   po·tray as·kol·tar·lo kwee

Photography

English	Italian	Pronunciation
I need a/an ...	Vorrei un rullino	vo·ray oon roo·lee·no
film for this	... per questa	... per kwe·sta
camera.	macchina	ma·kee·na
	fotografica.	fo·to·gra·fee·ka
APS	da APS	da a·pee·e·se
B&W	in bianco e nero	een byan·ko e ne·ro
colour	a colori	a ko·lo·ree
(200) speed	da (duecento)	da (doo·e chen·to)
	ASA	a·za
Could you ...?	Potrebbe ...?	po·tre·be ...
develop this	sviluppare	svee·loo·pa·re
film	questo rullino	kwe·sto roo·lee·no
load my film	inserire il	een·se·ree·re eel
	mio rullino	mee·o roo·lee·no

How much is it to develop this film?

Quanto costa sviluppare kwan·to kos·ta svee·loo·pa·re
questo rullino? kwe·sto roo·lee·no

When will it be ready?

Quando sarà pronto? kwan·do sa·ra pron·to

Do you have one-hour processing?

Si offre il servizio see o·fre eel ser·vee·tsyo
sviluppo e stampa in svee·loo·po e stam·pa een
un ora? oon o·ra

I'm not happy with these photos.

Non mi piacciono non mee pya·cho·no
queste foto. kwe·ste fo·to

ENJOY
What's on?

What's on ...?	Che c'è in programma ...?	ke che een pro·gra·ma ...
locally	in zona	een dzo·na
this	questo fine	kwe·sto fee·ne
weekend	settimana	se·tee·ma·na
today	oggi	o·jee
tonight	stasera	sta·se·ra
Where are the ...?	Dove sono ...?	do·ve so·no ...
clubs	dei clubs	day kloob
gay hangouts	dei locali gay	day lo·ka·lee gei
places to eat	i posti in cui mangiare	ee pos·tee een koo·ee man·ja·re
pubs	dei pub	day poob
Is there a local ... guide?	C'è una guida ... in questa città?	che oo·na gwee·da ... een kwe·sta chee·ta
entertainment	agli spettacoli	a·lyee spe·ta·ko·lee
film	ai film	ai feelm
I feel like going to ...	Ho voglia d'andare ...	o vo·lya dan·da·re ...
the ballet	a un balletto	a oon ba·le·to
a bar	a un locale	a oon lo·ka·le
a café	a un bar	a oon bar
a concert	a un concerto	a oon kon·cher·to
a nightclub	in un locale notturno	een oon lo·ka·le no·toor·no
the opera	all'opera	a·lo·pe·ra
a restaurant	in un ristorante	een oon rees·to·ran·te
the theatre	a teatro	a te·a·tro

Meeting up

What time shall we meet?
A che ora ci vediamo?　　　　a ke *o*·ra chee ve·*dya*·mo

Where will we meet?
Dove ci vediamo?　　　　　　*do*·ve chee ve·*dya*·mo

Let's meet at …	*Incontriamoci …*	een·kon·*trya*·mo·chee …
(eight) o'clock	*alle (otto)*	*a*·le (*o*·to)
the entrance	*all'entrata*	a·len·*tra*·ta

Small talk

What do you do in your spare time?
Cosa fai nel tuo tempo　　　*ko*·za fai nel *too*·o tem·po
libero?　　　　　　　　　　　*lee*·be·ro

Do you like to …?	*Ti piace …?*	tee pya·che …
I (don't) like to …	*(Non) Mi piace …*	(non) mee *pya*·che…
dance	*ballare*	ba·*la*·re
go to concerts	*andare ai*	an·*da*·re ai
	concerti	kon·*cher*·tee
listen to music	*ascoltare la*	as·kol·*ta*·re la
	musica	*moo*·zee·ka

I (don't) like …	*(Non) mi piacciono …*	(non) mee *pya*·cho·no …
action movies	*i film d'azione*	ee feelm da·*tsyo*·ne
Italian films	*i film*	ee feelm
	italiani	ee·tal·*ya*·nee
sci-fi films	*i film di*	ee feelm dee
	fantascienza	fan·ta·*shen*·tsa

EAT & DRINK

breakfast	*prima colazione* f	*pree*·ma ko·la·*tsyo*·ne
lunch	*pranzo* m	*pran*·dzo
dinner	*cena* f	*che*·na
snack	*spuntino* m	spoon·*tee*·no

Choosing & booking

Where would you go for a celebration?
Dove andrebbe per   *do*·ve an·*dre*·be per
una celebrazione?   *oo*·na che·le·bra·*tsyo*·ne

Can you recommend a ...	*Potrebbe consigliare un ...*	po·*tre*·be kon·see·*lya*·re oon ...
bar	*locale*	lo·*ka*·le
café	*bar*	bar
restaurant	*ristorante*	rees·to·*ran*·te

Where would you go for ...?	*Dove andrebbe per ...*	*do*·ve an·*dre*·be per ...
a cheap meal	*un pasto economico*	oon *pas*·to e·ko·*no*·mee·ko
local specialities	*le specialità locali*	le spe·cha·lee·*ta* lo·*ka*·lee

I'd like ..., please.	*Vorrei ..., per favore.*	vo·*ray* ... per fa·*vo*·re
a table for (four)	*un tavolo per (quattro)*	oon *ta*·vo·lo per (*kwa*·tro)
the (non) smoking section	*(non) fumatori*	(non) foo·ma·*to*·ree

EAT & DRINK

Eateries

With such a diverse selection of fantastic places to eat, you'll never go hungry in Italy. Sample the local flavour at some of these cheap and cheerful eateries:

bar/caffè bar/ka·fe
a café that serves drinks but also offers light meals such as bread rolls and snacks

osteria/trattoria os·te·ree·a/tra·to·ree·a
a local eatery providing simple food and regional specialities

paninoteca pa·nee·no·te·ka
a snack shop that serves delicious sandwiches made with cheese and cold meats

tavola calda ta·vo·la kal·da
a buffet offering local specialities, pizza, roasted meats and salads

pizzeria pee·tse·ree·a
a cheap restaurant specialising in pizza and calzoni (a folded pizza dish), usually prepared in a woodfired oven

ristorante ree·sto·ran·te
a sophisticated eatery – expect a high standard of service, a more expensive menu and an extensive winelist

Ordering

What would you recommend?
   Cosa mi consiglia?   ko·za mee kon·see·lya

I'd like …, please.	*Vorrei …, per favore.*	vo·ray … per fa·vo·re
the bill	*il conto*	eel kon·to
the menu	*il menù*	eel me·noo
the wine list	*la lista dei vini*	la lee·sta day vee·nee

I'd like ..., please.	Vorrei ..., per favore.	vo·ray ... per fa·vo·re
the chicken	il pollo	eel po·lo
a napkin	un tovagliolo	oon to·va·lyo·lo
pepper	il pepe	eel pe·pe
salt	il sale	eel sa·le
the set menu	il menù fisso	eel me·noo fee·so
I'd like it ...	Lo vorrei ...	lo vo·ray ...
medium	non troppo cotto	non tro·po ko·to
rare	al sangue	al san·gwe
well-done	ben cotto	ben ko·to
without sauce/	senza salsa/	sen·tsa sal·sa/
dressing	condimento	kon·dee·men·to

Nonalcoholic drinks

(cup of) coffee	(un) caffè m	(oon) ka·fe
(cup of) tea	(un) tè m	(oon) te
... with milk	... con latte	... kon la·te
... without/	... senza/con	... sen·tsa/kon
with (sugar)	(zucchero)	(tsoo·ke·ro)
orange juice (bottled)	succo m d'arancia	soo·ko da·ran·cha
orange juice (fresh)	spremuta f d'arancia	spre·moo·ta da·ran·cha
soft drink	bibita f	bee·bee·ta
... water	acqua f ...	a·kwa ...
hot	calda	kal·da
sparkling mineral	frizzante	free·tsan·te
still mineral	naturale	na·too·ra·le

Caffè della casa

Love the smell of coffee in the morning? Italy is a caffeine-addict's dream with more ways of making the humble brew than you can shake a spoon at:

caffè alla valdostana   *ka·fe a·la val·dos·ta·na*
with grappa, lemon peel and spices

caffè americano   *ka·fe a·me·ree·ka·no*
long and black

caffè corretto   *ka·fe ko·re·to*
with a dash of liqueur

caffè doppio   *ka·fe do·pyo*
long, strong and black

caffè macchiato   *ka·fe ma·kya·to*
strong with a drop of milk

caffè ristretto   *ka·fe ree·stre·to*
short, black and super strong

caffellate   *ka·fe·la·te*
with milk – usually consumed at breakfast

cappuccino   *ka·poo·chee·no*
prepared with milk, served with a lot of froth – considered a morning drink

espresso   *es·pre·so*
short black

Alcoholic drinks

beer	*birra* f	*bee·ra*
brandy	*cognac* m	*ko·nyak*
champagne	*champagne* m	*sham·pa·nye*
cocktail	*cocktail* m	*kok·tayl*

a ... of beer	... di birra	... dee *bee*·ra
bottle	*una bottiglia*	*oo*·na bo·*tee*·lya
glass	*un bicchiere*	oon bee·*kye*·re
a bottle of	*una bottiglia*	*oo*·na bo·*tee*·lya
... wine	*di vino ...*	dee *vee*·no ...
a glass of	*un bicchiere*	oon bee·*kye*·re
... wine	*di vino ...*	dee *vee*·no ...
red	*rosso*	*ro*·so
sparkling	*spumante*	spoo·*man*·te
white	*bianco*	*byan*·ko

a shot of (whisky)
un sorso di (whisky)   oon *sor*·so dee (*wee*·skee)

In the bar

I'll have (a gin).	*Prendo (un gin).*	*pren*·do (oon jeen)
Same again, please.	*Un altro, per favore.*	oo·*nal*·tro per fa·*vo*·re
I'll buy you a drink.	*Ti offro da bere.*	tee *of*·ro da *be*·re
What would you like?	*Cosa prendi?*	*ko*·za *pren*·dee
It's my round.	*Offro io.*	*of*·ro *ee*·o
Cheers!	*Salute!*	sa·*loo*·te

Buying food

What's the local speciality?
    Qual'è la specialità   kwa·*le* la spe·cha·lee·*ta*
    di questa regione?   dee *kwe*·sta re·*jo*·ne

What's that?
    Cos'è?   ko·*ze*

How much is (a kilo)?
Quanto costa (un chilo)?   kwan·to kos·ta (oon kee·lo)

I'd like some of that.
Mi piacerebbe un po' di quello.   mee pya·che·re·be oon po dee kwe·lo

I'd like some of those.
Vorrei un po' di quelli.   vo·ray oon po di kwe·lee

I'd like ...	*Vorrei ...*	vo·ray ...
100g	*un etto*	oo·ne·to
(two) kilos	*(due) chili*	*(doo·e) kee·lee*
(three) pieces	*(tre) pezzi*	(tre) pe·tsee
(six) slices	*(sei) fette*	(say) fe·te

Enough, thanks.
Basta, grazie.   bas·ta gra·tsye

A bit more, please.
Un po' di più, per favore.   oon po dee pyoo per fa·vo·re

Less, please.
Meno, per favore.   me·no per fa·vo·re

Special diets & allergies

Is there a (vegetarian) restaurant near here?
C'è un ristorante   che oon rees·to·ran·te
(vegetariano) qui vicino?   (ve·je·ta·rya·no) kwee vee·chee·no

Do you have (vegetarian) food?
Avete piatti (vegetariani)?   a·ve·te pya·tee (ve·je·ta·rya·nee)

Could you prepare	*Potreste preparare*	po·tres·te pre·pa·ra·re
a meal without ...?	*un pasto senza ...?*	oon pas·to sen·tsa ...
butter	*burro*	boo·ro
eggs	*uova*	wo·va
meat stock	*brodo di carne*	bro·do dee kar·ne

I'm ...	Sono ...	so·no ...
vegan	vegetaliano/a m/f	ve·je·ta·lya·no/a
vegetarian	vegetariano/a m/f	ve·je·ta·rya·no/a

I'm allergic to ...	Sono allergico/a ... m/f	so·no a·ler·jee·ko/a ...
caffeine	alla caffeina	a·la ka·fe·yee·na
dairy produce	ai latticini	ai la·tee·chee·nee
eggs	alle uova	a·le wo·va
gluten	al glutine	al gloo·tee·ne
nuts	alle noci	a·le no·chee
seafood	ai frutti di mare	ai froo·tee dee ma·re

For more on allergies see **HELP**, page 66 and **LOOK UP**, page 70.

On the menu

EAT & DRINK

Antipasti	an·tee·pas·tee	appetisers
Zuppe	tsoo·pe	soups
Primi (piatti)	pree·mee (pya·tee)	entrees
Insalate	een·sa·la·te	salads
Secondi (piatti)	se·kon·dee (pya·tee)	main courses
Dolci	dol·chee	desserts
Bevande	be·van·de	drinks
Aperitivi	a·pe·ree·tee·vee	aperitifs
Liquori	lee·kwo·ree	spirits
Birre	bee·re	beers
Vini Frizzanti	vee·nee free·tsan·tee	sparkling wines
Vini Bianchi	vee·nee byan·kee	white wines
Vini Rossi	vee·nee ro·see	red wines
Vini da Dessert	vee·nee da de·sert	dessert wines

For more help reading the menu, see the **Menu decoder** on the next page.

Menu decoder

acciughe f pl	a·*choo*·ge	anchovies
aceto m	a·*che*·to	vinegar
affumicato/a m/f	a·foo·mee·*ka*·to/a	smoked
aglio m	a·lyo	garlic
agnello m	a·*nye*·lo	lamb
al dente	al *den*·te	'to the tooth' – describes cooked pasta & rice that are still slightly hard
al forno	al *for*·no	cooked in an oven
al sangue	al *san*·gwe	rare
al vapore	al va·*po*·re	steamed
alla diavola	a·la *dya*·vo·la	spicy dish
alla napoletana	a·la na·po·le·*ta*·na	from or in the style of Naples – usually includes tomatoes & garlic
all'amatriciana	al a·ma·tree·*cha*·na	spicy sauce with salami, tomato, capsicums & cheese
all'arrabbiata	al a·ra·*bya*·ta	'angry-style' – with spicy sauce
antipasto m	an·tee·*pas*·to	appetizers • hors d'oeuvres
aragosta f	a·ra·*go*·sta	lobster • crayfish
arancini m pl	a·ran·*chee*·nee	rice balls stuffed with a meat mixture
aringa f	a·*reen*·ga	herring
arista f	a·*ree*·sta	cured, cooked pork meat

aromi m pl	a·*ro*·mee	aromatic herbs • spices
babà m	ba·*ba*	dessert containing sultanas
baccalà m	ba·ka·*la*	dried salted cod
baci m pl	*ba*·chee	'kisses' – type of chocolate • type of pastry or biscuit
bagna f *cauda*	*ban*·ya *cow*·da	anchovy, olive oil & garlic dip served with raw vegetables
basilico m	ba·*zee*·lee·ko	basil
ben cotto/a m/f	ben *ko*·to/a	well done
besciamella f	be·sha·*me*·la	white sauce
bistecca f	bees·*te*·ka	steak
bollito/a m/f	bo·*lee*·to/a	boiled
braciola f	bra·*cho*·la	chop
brioche m	bree·*osh*	breakfast pastry
brodo m	*bro*·do	broth
bruschetta f	broos·*ke*·ta	toasted bread with olive oil & various toppings
budino m	boo·*dee*·no	milk-based pudding
busecca f	boo·*ze*·ka	tripe
cacciucco m	ka·*choo*·ko	seafood stew with wine, garlic & herbs
calzone m	kal·*tso*·ne	fried or baked flat bread made with two thin sheets of pasta stuffed with any number of ingredients
cannella f	ka·*ne*·la	cinnamon

cannelloni m pl	ka·ne·*lo*·nee	tubes of pasta stuffed with spinach, minced roast veal, ham, eggs, parmesan & spices
cantarelli m pl	kan·ta·*re*·lee	chanterelle mushrooms
cantucci m pl	kan·*too*·chee	crunchy, hard biscuits made with aniseed & almonds
caponata f	ka·po·*na*·ta	eggplant with a tomato sauce
carciofi m pl	kar·*cho*·fee	artichokes
ciabatta f	cha·*ba*·ta	crisp, flat & long bread
cioccolato m	cho·ko·*la*·to	chocolate
coda f	*ko*·da	tail • angler fish
conchiglie f pl	kon·*kee*·lye	pasta shells
condimento m	kon·dee·*men*·to	condiment • seasoning • dressing
contorni m pl	kon·*tor*·nee	side dishes • vegetables
costine f pl	kos·*tee*·ne	ribs
cozze f pl	*ko*·tse	mussels
crespella f	kres·*pe*·la	thin fritter
crostata f	kro·*sta*·ta	fruit tart • crust
crostini m pl	kro·*stee*·nee	slices of bread toasted with savoury toppings
crudo/a m/f	*kroo*·do/a	raw
della casa	*de*·la *ka*·za	'of the house' – house speciality
dolce m	*dol*·che	dessert • sweet
erbe f pl	*er*·be	herbs
fagiano m	fa·*ja*·no	pheasant

fagioli m pl	fa·*jo*·lee	beans
farcito/a m/f	far·*chee*·to/a	stuffed
farfalle f pl	far·*fa*·le	butterfly-shaped pasta
farinata f	fa·ree·*na*·ta	thin, flat bread made from chickpea flour
fetta f	*fe*·ta	a slice
fettuccine f pl	fe·too·*chee*·ne	long ribbon-shaped pasta
filetto m	fee·*le*·to	fillet
focaccia f	fo·*ka*·cha	flat bread often filled/topped with cheese, ham, vegetables & other ingredients
formaggio m	for·*ma*·jo	cheese
fragole f pl	*fra*·go·le	strawberries
fresco/a m/f	*fres*·ko/a	fresh
frittata f	free·*ta*·ta	thick omelette slice, served hot or cold
frittelle f pl	free·*te*·le	fritters
fritto/a m/f	*free*·to/a	fried
frumento m	froo·*men*·to	wheat
frutta f	*froo*·ta	fruit
frutti m pl *di mare*	*froo*·tee dee *ma*·re	sea food
funghi m pl	*foon*·gee	mushrooms
gambero m	*gam*·be·ro	prawn • shrimp
gamberoni m pl	gam·be·*ro*·nee	prawns
gelato m	je·*la*·to	ice cream
gnocchi m pl	*nyo*·kee	small dumplings – most commonly potato dumplings

gorgonzola f	gor·gon·*dzo*·la	spicy, sweet, creamy blue vein cow's milk cheese
granita f	gra·*nee*·ta	finely crushed flavoured ice
grappa f	*gra*·pa	distilled grape must
insalata f	een·sa·*la*·ta	salad
involtini m pl	een·vol·*tee*·nee	stuffed rolls of meat or fish
lenticchie f pl	len·*tee*·kye	lentils
lievito m	*lye*·vee·to	yeast
limone m	lee·*mo*·ne	lemon
lingua f	*leen*·gwa	tongue
linguine f pl	leen·*gwee*·ne	long thin ribbons of pasta
luganega f	loo·*ga*·ne·ga	pork sausage
lumache f pl	loo·*ma*·ke	snails
maccheroni m pl	ma·ke·*ro*·nee	any tube pasta
marinato/a m/f	ma·ree·*na*·to/a	marinated
mascarpone m	mas·kar·*po*·ne	very soft & creamy cheese
melanzane f pl	me·lan·*dza*·ne	eggplants • aubergines
minestra f	mee·*ne*·stra	general word for soup
minestrone m	mee·ne·*stro*·ne	traditional vegetable soup
misto/a m/f	*mees*·to/a	mixed
noce m	*no*·che	nut • walnut
non troppo cotto/a m/f	non *tro*·po *ko*·to/a	medium rare
olio m	*o*·lyo	oil – almost always olive oil
ossobuco m	o·so·*boo*·ko	veal shanks
ostriche f pl	*os*·tree·ke	oysters
pancetta f	pan·*che*·ta	salt-cured bacon
pane m	*pa*·ne	bread
panino m	pa·*nee*·no	bread roll

panzanella f	pan·tsa·*ne*·la	tomato, onion, garlic, olive oil, bread & basil salad
patate f pl	pa·*ta*·te	potatoes
pecorino m (romano)	pe·ko·*ree*·no (ro·*ma*·no)	hard & spicy cheese made from ewe's milk
penne f pl	*pe*·ne	short & tubular pasta
peperoncini m pl	pe·pe·ron·*chee*·nee	hot chilli
peperoni m pl	pe·pe·*ro*·nee	peppers • capsicum
pesto m	*pes*·to	paste made from garlic, basil, pine nuts & Parmesan
poco cotto/a m/f	*po*·ko *ko*·to/a	rare
polenta f	po·*len*·ta	corn meal porridge
polpette m	pol·*pe*·te	meatballs
pomodori m pl	po·mo·*do*·ree	tomatoes
prosciutto m	pro·*shoo*·to	basic name for many types of thinly-sliced ham
quattro formaggi	*kwa*·tro for·*ma*·jee	pasta sauce with four different cheeses
quattro stagioni	*kwa*·tro sta·*jo*·nee	pizza with different toppings on each quarter
ragù m	ra·*goo*	generally a meat sauce but sometimes vegetarian
ravioli m pl	ra·vee·*o*·lee	pasta squares usually stuffed with meat, parmesan cheese & breadcrumbs
rigatoni m pl	ree·ga·*to*·nee	short, fat tubes of pasta
ripieno m	ree·*pye*·no	stuffing
riso m	*ree*·zo	rice

risotto m	ree-*zo*-to	rice dish slowly cooked in broth to a creamy consistency
rucola f	*roo*-ko-la	rocket
salsa f	*sal*-sa	sauce
salsiccia f	sal-*see*-cha	sausage
spaghetti m pl	spa-*ge*-tee	ubiquitous long thin strands of pasta
spalla f	*spa*-la	shoulder
speck m	spek	type of smoked ham
suppa f	*soo*-pa	soup
tacchino m	ta-*kee*-no	turkey
tagliatelle f	ta-lya-*te*-le	long, ribbon-shaped pasta
tartufo m	tar-*too*-fo	truffle (very expensive kind of mushroom)
tiramisù m	tee-ra-mee-*soo*	sponge cake soaked in coffee & arranged in layers with mascarpone, then sprinkled with cocoa
torta f	*tor*-ta	cake • tart • pie
tortellini m pl	tor-te-*lee*-nee	pasta filled with meat, parmesan & egg
uova m pl	*wo*-va	eggs
uva f pl	*oo*-va	grapes
verdure f pl	ver-*doo*-re	vegetables
vino m *della casa*	*vee*-no de-la *ka*-sa	house wine
vitello m	vee-*te*-lo	veal
vongole f pl	*von*-go-le	clams
zucca f	*tsoo*-ka	pumpkin
zucchero m	*tsoo*-ke-ro	sugar
zuppa f	*tsoo*-pa	soup

EAT & DRINK

41

SERVICES
Post office

I want to send a ...	*Vorrei mandare un/una ...* m/f	vo·*ray* man·*da*·re oon/*oo*·na ...
fax	*fax* m	faks
letter	*lettera* f	*le*·te·ra
parcel	*pacchetto* m	pa·*ke*·to
postcard	*cartolina* f	kar·to·*lee*·na
I want to buy ...	*Vorrei comprare ...*	vo·*ray* kom·*pra*·re ...
an aerogram	*un aerogramma*	oo·na·e·ro·*gra*·ma
an envelope	*una busta*	*oo*·na *boo*·sta
stamps	*dei francobolli*	day fran·ko·*bo*·lee
Please send it (to Australia) by ...	*Lo mandi ... (in Australia), per favore.*	lo *man*·dee ... (ee·now·*stra*·lya) per fa·*vo*·re
airmail	*via aerea*	*vee*·a a·e·re·a
express mail	*posta prioritaria*	*pos*·ta pryo·ree·*ta*·rya
regular mail	*posta ordinaria*	*pos*·ta or·dee·*na*·rya
sea mail	*via* f *mare*	*vee*·a *ma*·re

Bank

Where's the nearest ...?	*Dov'è ... più vicino?*	do·*ve* ... pyoo vee·*chee*·no
automatic teller machine	*il Bancomat*	eel *ban*·ko·mat
foreign exchange office	*il cambio*	eel *kam*·byo

I'd like to ...	Vorrei ...	vo·ray ...
Where can I ...?	Dove posso ...?	do·ve po·so ...
arrange a transfer	trasferire	tras·fe·ree·re
	soldi	sol·dee
cash a cheque	riscuotere	ree·skwo·te·re
	un assegno	oo·na·se·nyo
change money	cambiare denaro	kam·bya·re de·na·ro
change a travellers	cambiare un	kam·bya·re
cheque	assegno	oo·na·se·nyo
	di viaggio	dee vee·a·jo
get a cash advance	prelevare con	pre·le·va·re kon
	carta di credito	kar·ta dee kre·dee·to
withdraw money	fare un prelievo	fa·re oon pre·lye·vo
What's the ...?	Quant'è ...?	kwan·te ...
commission	la commissione	la ko·mee·syo·ne
exchange rate	il cambio	eel kam·byo

What's the charge for that?
Quanto costa?   kwan·to kos·ta

What time does the bank open?
A che ora apre la banca?   a ke o·ra a·pre la ban·ka

Phone

What's your phone number?
Qual'è il Suo/tuo numero   kwa·le eel soo·o/too·o noo·me·ro
di telefono? pol/inf   dee te·le·fo·no

Where's the nearest public phone?
Dov'è il telefono pubblico   do·ve eel te·le·fo·no poo·blee·ko
più vicino?   pyoo vee·chee·no

I want to make a ...	Vorrei fare ...	vo·ray fa·re ...
call	una chiamata	oo·na kya·ma·ta
local call	una chiamata locale	oo·na kya·ma·ta lo·ka·le
reverse-charge/ collect call	una chiamata a carico del destinatario	oo·na kya·ma·ta a ka·ree·ko del des·tee·na·ta·ryo
How much does ... cost?	Quanto costa ...?	kwan·to kos·ta ...
a (three)-minute call	una telefonata di (tre) minuti	oo·na te·le·fo·na·ta dee (tre) mee·noo·tee
each extra minute	ogni minuto in più	o·nyee mee·noo·to een pyoo

I'd like to buy a phonecard.

Vorrei comprare una scheda telefonica.

vo·ray kom·pra·re oo·na ske·da te·le·fo·nee·ka

The number is ...

Il numero è ...

eel noo·me·ro e ...

Can I speak to ...?

Posso parlare con ...?

po·so par·la·re kon ...

Please tell him/her I called.

Gli/Le dica che ho telefonato, per favore.

lyee/le dee·ka ke o te·le·fo·na·to per fa·vo·re

Mobile/cell phone

What are the rates?

Quali sono le tariffe?

kwa·lee so·no le ta·ree·fe

(30c) per (30) seconds.

(Trenta centesimi) per (trenta) secondi.

(tren·ta chen·te·zee·mee) per (tren·ta) se·kon·dee

I'd like a/an …	Vorrei …	vo·ray …
adaptor plug	un adattatore	oo·na·da·ta·to·re
charger for	un carica-	oon ka·ree·ka·
my phone	batterie	ba·te·ree·e
mobile phone/	un cellulare da	oon che·loo·la·re da
cellphone for hire	noleggiare	no·le·ja·re
prepaid mobile	un cellulare	oon che·loo·la·re
phone/cellphone	prepagato	pre·pa·ga·to
SIM card for your	un SIM card per la	oon seem kard per la
network	rete telefonica	re·te te·le·fo·nee·ka

Internet

Where's the local Internet café?
Dove si trova l'Internet point?   do·ve see tro·va leen·ter·net poynt

How much per hour?
Quanto costa all'ora?   kwan·to kos·ta a·lo·ra

How much per page?
Quanto costa a pagina?   kwan·to kos·ta a pa·jee·na

Can you help me change to English-language preference?
Mi può aiutare a cambiare   mee pwo ai·yoo·ta·re a kam·bya·re
la lingua in inglese   la leen·gwa een een·gle·ze

It's crashed.
Si è bloccato.   see e blo·ka·to

I'd like to …	Vorrei …	vo·ray …
check my email	controllare le	kon·tro·la·re le
	mie email	mee·e e·mayl
get Internet access	usare Internet	oo·za·re een·ter·net
use a printer	usare una	oo·za·re oo·na
	stampante	stam·pan·te

45

GO
Directions

Where's the ...?	Dov'è ...?	do·ve ...
bank	la banca	la ban·ka
hotel	l'albergo	lal·ber·go
police station	il posto di polizia	eel pos·to dee po·lee·tsee·a

Can you show me (on the map)?
Può mostrarmi (sulla pianta)?   pwo mos·trar·mee (soo·la pyan·ta)

What's the address?
Qual'è l'indirizzo?   kwa·le leen·dee·ree·tso

How do I get there?
Come ci si arriva?   ko·me chee see a·ree·va

How far is it?
Quant'è distante?   kwan·te dees·tan·te

It's ...	È ...	e ...
behind ...	dietro ...	dye·tro ...
far away	lontano	lon·ta·no
here	qui	kwee
in front of ...	davanti a ...	da·van·tee a ...
left	a sinistra	a see·nee·stra
near (to ...)	vicino (a ...)	vee·chee·no (a ...)
next to ...	accanto a ...	a·kan·to a ...
on the corner	all'angolo	a lan·go·lo
opposite ...	di fronte a ...	dee fron·te a ...
right	a destra	a de·stra
straight ahead	sempre diritto	sem·pre dee·ree·to
there	là	la

It's ...	È a ...	e a ...
(100) metres	(cento) metri	(chen·to) me·tree
(10) minutes	(dieci) minuti	(dye·chee) mee·noo·tee

Turn ...	Giri ...	jee·ree ...
at the corner	all'angolo	a·lan·go·lo
at the traffic lights	al semaforo	al se·ma·fo·ro
left	a sinistra	a see·nee·stra
right	a destra	a de·stra

by bus	con l'autobus	kon low·to·boos
on foot	a piedi	a pye·dee
by metro	con la metropolitana	kon la me·tro·po·lee·ta·na
by taxi	con il tassì	ko·neel ta·see
by train	con il treno	ko·neel tre·no

north	al nord	al nord
south	al sud	al sood
east	all'est	al·est
west	all'ovest	al·o·vest

GO

Getting around

What time does the ... leave?	A che ora parte ...?	a ke o·ra par·te ...
boat	la nave	la na·ve
bus	l'autobus	low·to·boos
metro	la metropolitana	la me·tro·po·lee·ta·na
plane	l'aereo	la·e·re·o
train	il treno	eel tre·no

What time's the ... bus?	A che ora passa ... autobus	a ke o·ra pa·sa ... ow·to·boos
first	il primo	eel pree·mo
last	l'ultimo	lool·tee·mo
next	il prossimo	eel pro·see·mo

How many stops to ...?
Quante fermate mancano ...?   kwan·te fer·ma·te man·ka·no ...

Is this seat free?
È libero questo posto?   e lee·be·ro kwe·sto pos·to

That's my seat.
Quel posto è mio.   kwel pos·to e mee·o

Can you tell me when we get to ...?
Mi sa dire quando arriviamo a ...?   mee sa dee·re kwan·do a·ree·vya·mo a ...

I want to get off ...	Voglio scendere ...	vo·lyo shen·de·re ...
at the Colosseum	al Colosseo	al ko·lo·se·o
here	qui	kwee

Tickets & luggage

Where can I buy a ticket?
Dove posso comprare un biglietto?   do·ve po·so kom·pra·re oon bee·lye·to

Do I need to book (a seat)?
Bisogna prenotare (un posto)?   bee·zo·nya pre·no·ta·re (oon pos·to)

How long does the trip take?
Quanto ci vuole?   kwan·to chee vwo·le

GO

I'd like to ... my ticket, please.	Vorrei ... il mio biglietto, per favore.	vo·*ray* ... eel *mee*·o bee·*lye*·to per fa·*vo*·re
cancel	cancellare	kan·che·*la*·re
change	cambiare	kam·*bya*·re
collect	ritirare	ree·tee·*ra*·re
confirm	confermare	kon·fer·*ma*·re

How much is it?	Quant'è?	kwan·*te*

One ... ticket (to Rome), please.	Un biglietto ... (per Roma), per favore.	oon bee·*lye*·to ... (per *ro*·ma) per fa·*vo*·re
1st-class	di prima classe	dee *pree*·ma *kla*·se
2nd-class	di seconda classe	dee se·*kon*·da *kla*·se
child's	per bambini	per bam·*bee*·nee
one-way	di sola andata	dee *so*·la an·*da*·ta
return	di andata e ritorno	dee an·*da*·ta e ree·*tor*·no
student's	per studenti	per stoo·*den*·tee

I'd like a/an ... seat, please.	Vorrei un posto ..., per favore.	vo·*ray* oon *pos*·to ... per fa·*vo*·re
aisle	sul corridoio	sool ko·ree·do·*do*·yo
nonsmoking	per non fumatori	per non foo·ma·*to*·ree
smoking	per fumatori	per foo·ma·*to*·ree
window	vicino al finestrino	vee·*chee*·no al fee·nes·*tree*·no

Is there air-conditioning?
C'è l'aria condizionata?   che *la*·rya kon·dee·*tsyo*·*na*·ta

Is there a toilet?
C'è un gabinetto?   che oon ga·bee·*ne*·to

49

Is it a direct route?
È un itinerario diretto?   e oo·nee·tee·ne·*ra*·ryo dee·*re*·to

What time do I have to check in?
A che ora devo presentarmi   a ke o·ra *de*·vo pre·zen·*tar*·mee
per l'accettazione?   per la·che·ta·*tsyo*·ne

Can I get a stand-by ticket?
Posso mettermi in   po·so *me*·ter·mee een
lista d'attesa?   *lees*·ta da·*te*·za

Where's the baggage claim?
Dov'è il ritiro bagagli?   do·*ve* eel ree·*tee*·ro ba·*ga*·lyee

I'd like a luggage locker.
Vorrei un armadietto   vo·*ray* oo·nar·ma·*dye*·to
per il bagaglio.   per eel ba·*ga*·lyo

Can I have some coins/tokens?
Può darmi della moneta/   pwo *dar*·mee *de*·la mo·*ne*·ta/
dei gettoni?   day je·*to*·nee

My luggage	*Il mio bagaglio*	eel *mee*·o ba·*ga*·lyo
has been ...	*è stato ...*	e *sta*·to ...
damaged	*danneggiato*	da·ne·*ja*·to
lost	*perso*	*per*·so
stolen	*rubato*	roo·*ba*·to

Bus, metro, taxi & train

Which bus goes to ...?
Quale autobus va a ...?   *kwa*·le *ow*·to·boos va a ...

Is this the bus to ...?
Questo autobus va a ...?   *kwe*·sto *ow*·to·boos va a ...

What station is this?
Che stazione è questa?   ke sta·*tsyo*·ne e *kwe*·sta

What's the next station?
Qual'è la prossima stazione?
kwa·*le* la *pro*·see·ma sta·*tsyo*·ne

Does this train stop at (Milan)?
Questo treno si ferma a (Milano)?
kwe·sto *tre*·no see *fer*·ma a (mee·*la*·no)

Do I need to change trains?
Devo cambiare treno?
de·vo kam·*bya*·re *tre*·no

Which carriage is for (Rome)?
Quale carrozza è per (Roma)?
kwa·le ka·*ro*·tsa e per (*ro*·ma)

Which carriage is (1st class)?
Quale carrozza è (di prima classe?)
kwa·le ka·*ro*·tsa e (dee *pree*·ma *kla*·se)

Where's the dining car?
Dov'è il vagone ristorante?
do·*ve* eel va·*go*·ne rees·to·*ran*·te

Where's the taxi stand?
Dov'è la fermata dei tassì?
do·*ve* la fer·*ma*·ta day ta·*see*

I'd like a taxi ...	*Vorrei un tassì ...*	vo·*ray* oon ta·*see* ...
at (9am)	*alle (nove di mattina)*	*a*·le (*no*·ve dee ma·*tee*·na)
now	*adesso*	a·*de*·so
tomorrow	*domani*	do·*ma*·nee

Is this taxi free?
È libero questo tassì?
e *lee*·be·ro *kwe*·sto ta·*see*

How much is it to ...?
Quant'è per ...?
kwan·*te* per ...

Please put the meter on.
Usi il tassametro, per favore.
oo·zee eel ta·sa·*me*·tro per fa·*vo*·re

GO

51

Please take me to (this address).

Mi porti a (questo indirizzo), per piacere.	mee *por*·tee a (*kwe*·sto een·dee·*ree*·tso) per pya·*che*·re

Please ...	..., per favore.	... per fa·*vo*·re
slow down	*Rallenti*	ra·*len*·tee
wait here	*Mi aspetti qui*	mee as·*pe*·tee kwee

Stop ...	*Si fermi ...*	see *fer*·mee ...
at the corner	*all'angolo*	a *lan*·go·lo
here	*qui*	kwee

Car & motorbike hire

I'd like to hire a ...	*Vorrei noleggiare ...*	vo·*ray* no·le·*ja*·re ...
(large/small) car	*una macchina (grande/piccola)*	*oo*·na *ma*·kee·na (*gran*·de/*pee*·ko·la)
motorbike	*una moto*	*oo*·na *mo*·to

with/without ...	*con/senza ...*	kon/*sen*·tsa ...
air-conditioning	*aria condizionata*	*a*·rya kon·dee·tsyo·*na*·ta
antifreeze	*anticongelante*	an·tee·kon·je·*lan*·te
snow chains	*le catene da neve*	le ka·*te*·ne da *ne*·ve

How much for ... hire?	*Quanto costa ...?*	*kwan*·to *kos*·ta ...
daily	*al giorno*	al *jor*·no
hourly	*all'ora*	a·*lo*·ra
weekly	*alla settimana*	*a*·la se·tee·*ma*·na

Does that include ...?	È compreso/a ... m/f	e kom·*pre*·zo/a ...
mileage	il chilometraggio m	eel kee·lo·me·*tra*·jo
insurance	l'assicurazione f	la·see·koo·ra·*tsyo*·ne

What's the speed limit?
Qual'è il limite di velocità? kwa·*le* eel *lee*·mee·te dee ve·lo·chee·*ta*

Is this the road to ...?
Questa strada porta a ...? *kwe*·sta *stra*·da *por*·ta a ...

Where's a service station?
Dov'è una stazione di servizio? do·*ve* oo·na sta·*tsyo*·ne dee ser·*vee*·tsyo

(How long) Can I park here?
(Per quanto tempo) Posso parcheggiare qui? (per kwan·to tem·po) *po*·so par·ke·*ja*·re kwee

| leaded | benzina f con piombo | ben·*dzee*·na kon *pyom*·bo |
| unleaded | benzina f senza piombo | ben·*dzee*·na *sen*·tsa *pyom*·bo |

GO

Road signs

Dare la Precedenza	*da*·re la pre·che·*den*·tsa	Give Way
Divieto di Accesso	dee·*vye*·to dee a·*che*·so	No Entry
Entrata	en·*tra*·ta	Entrance
Pedaggio	pe·*da*·jo	Toll
Senso Unico	*sen*·so oo·nee·ko	One Way
Stop	stop	Stop
Uscita	oo·*shee*·ta	Exit

SLEEP
Finding accommodation

Where's a/an ...?	Dov'è ...?	do·ve ...
bed & breakfast	un bed e breakfast	oon bed e brek·fast
camping ground	un campeggio	oon kam·pe·jo
guesthouse	una pensione	oo·na pen·syo·ne
hotel	un albergo	oo·nal·ber·go
inn (budget hotel)	una locanda	oo·na lo·kan·da
room	una camera	oo·na ka·me·ra
youth hostel	un ostello della gioventù	oo·nos·te·lo de·la jo·ven·too

Can you recommend somewhere ...?	Può consigliare qualche posto ...?	pwo kon·see·lya·re kwal·ke pos·to ...
cheap	economico	e·ko·no·mee·ko
good	buono	bwo·no
luxurious	di lusso	dee loo·so
nearby	vicino	vee·chee·no
romantic	romantico	ro·man·tee·ko

What's the address?
Qual'è l'indirizzo?   kwa·le leen·dee·ree·tso

How do I get there?
Come ci si arriva?   ko·me chee see a·ree·va

For responses, see **GO**, page 46.

SLEEP

54

Booking ahead & checking in

I'd like to book a room, please.
Vorrei prenotare una camera,
per favore.
vo·*ray* pre·no·*ta*·re oo·na *ka*·me·ra
per fa·*vo*·re

I have a reservation.
Ho una prenotazione.
o oo·na pre·no·ta·*tsyo*·ne

My name's ...
Mi chiamo ...
mee *kya*·mo ...

Do you have a	*Avete una*	a·*ve*·te oo·na
... room?	*camera ...?*	*ka*·me·ra ...
double	*doppia con letto*	do·*pya* kon le·*to*
	matrimoniale	ma·tree·mo·*nya*·le
single	*singola*	*seen*·go·la
twin	*doppia a*	do·pya a
	due letti	doo·e le·tee

How much is it	*Quanto costa*	*kwan*·to *kos*·ta
per ...?	*per ...?*	per ...
night	*una notte*	oo·na *no*·te
person	*persona*	per·*so*·na
week	*una settimana*	oo·na se·tee·*ma*·na

I'd like to stay for (two) nights.
Vorrei rimanere
(due) notti.
vo·*ray* ree·ma·*ne*·re
(*doo*·e) *no*·tee

From (July 2) to (July 6).
Dal (due luglio) al (sei luglio).
dal (*doo*·e *loo*·lyo) al (say *loo*·lyo)

There are (three) of us.
Siamo (tre).
sya·mo (tre)

Can I see it?
Posso vederla? po·so ve·*der*·la

It's fine. I'll take it.
Va bene. La prendo. va *be*·ne la *pren*·do

Do I need to pay upfront?
Devo pagare in anticipo? de·vo pa·*ga*·re ee·nan·*tee*·chee·po

Can I pay ...?	*Posso pagare con ...?*	po·so pa·*ga*·re kon ...
by credit card	la carta di credito	la *kar*·ta dee *kre*·dee·to
with a travellers cheque	un assegno di viaggio	oo·na·*se*·nyo dee vee·*a*·jo

For methods of payment, see also **PAYING**, page 22 and **BANK**, page 42.

Requests & queries

When's breakfast served?
A che ora è la prima colazione? a ke *o*·ra e la *pree*·ma ko·la·*tsyo*·ne

Where's breakfast served?
Dove si prende la prima colazione? *do*·ve see *pren*·de la *pree*·ma ko·la·*tsyo*·ne

Please wake me at (seven).
Mi svegli (alle sette), per favore. mee *sve*·lyee (*a*·le *se*·te) per fa·*vo*·re

Could I have my key, please?
Può darmi la mia chiave, per favore? pwo *dar*·mee la *mee*·a *kya*·ve per fa·*vo*·re

Could I have a receipt, please?
Può darmi una ricevuta, per favore? pwo *dar*·mee *oo*·na ree·che·*voo*·ta per fa·*vo*·re

Can I use the ...?	Posso usare ...?	po·so oo·za·re ...
kitchen	la cucina	la koo·chee·na
laundry	la lavanderia	la la·van·de·ree·a
telephone	il telefono	eel te·le·fo·no

Do you have a/an ...?	C'è ...?	che ...
elevator	un ascensore	oo·na·shen·so·re
laundry service	il servizio	eel ser·vee·tsyo
	lavanderia	la·van·de·ree·a
safe	una cassaforte	oo·na ka·sa·for·te
swimming pool	una piscina	oo·na pee·shee·na

Do you arrange tours here?
Si organizzano le gite qui? see or·ga·nee·dza·no le jee·te kwee

Do you change money here?
Si cambiano i soldi qui? see kam·bya·no ee sol·dee kwee

The room is too ...	La camera è troppo ...	la ka·me·ra e tro·po ...
cold	fredda	fre·da
dark	scura	skoo·ra
expensive	cara	ka·ra
light/bright	luminosa	loo·mee·no·za
noisy	rumorosa	roo·mo·ro·za
small	piccola	pee·ko·la

The ... doesn't work.	... non funziona.	... non foon·tsyo·na
air-conditioning	L'aria condizionata	la·rya kon·dee·tsyo·na·ta
fan	Il ventilatore	eel ven·tee·la·to·re
toilet	Il gabinetto	eel ga·bee·ne·to
window	La finestra	la fee·nes·tra

SLEEP

57

Can I get another ...?	*Può darmi un altro/a ...* m/f	pwo *dar*·mee oo·*nal*·tro/a
This ... isn't clean.	*Questo/a ... non è pulito/a.* m/f	*kwe*·sto/a ... non e poo·*lee*·to/a
blanket	*coperta* f	ko·*per*·ta
pillow	*cuscino* m	koo·*shee*·no
pillowcase	*federa* f	*fe*·de·ra
towel	*asciugamano* m	a·shoo·ga·*ma*·no

Checking out

What time is checkout?
A che ora si deve lasciar libera la camera?
a ke o·*ra* see *de*·ve la·*shar lee*·be·ra la *ka*·me·ra

Can I leave my luggage here until ....?	*Posso lasciare il mio bagaglio qui fino ...?*	*po*·so la·*sha*·re eel *mee*·o ba·*ga*·lyo kwee *fee*·no ...
next week	*alla settimana prossima*	*a*·la se·tee·*ma*·na *pro*·see·ma
tonight	*a stasera*	a sta·*se*·ra
Wednesday	*a mercoledì*	a mer·ko·le·*dee*

Could I have my ..., please?	*Posso avere ..., per favore?*	*po*·so a·*ve*·re ... per fa·*vo*·re
deposit	*la caparra*	la ka·*pa*·ra
passport	*il mio passaporto*	eel *mee*·o pa·sa·*por*·to
valuables	*i miei oggetti di valore*	ee myay o·*je*·tee dee va·*lo*·re

I'll be back ...	*Torno ...*	*tor*·no ...
in (three) days	*fra (tre) giorni*	fra (tre) *jor*·nee
on (Tuesday)	*(martedì)*	(mar·te·*dee*)

SLEEP

58

WORK
Introductions

I'm attending a …	*Sono qui per un/una … m/f*	*so·no kwee per oon/oo·na …*
Where's the …?	*Dov'è il/la …? m/f*	*do·ve eel/la …*
business centre	*business centre m*	*beez·nees sen·ter*
conference	*conferenza f*	*kon·fe·ren·tsa*
course	*corso m*	*kor·so*
meeting	*riunione f*	*ree·oo·nyo·ne*
trade fair	*fiera f commerciale*	*fye·ra ko·mer·cha·le*
I'm here with …	*Sono qui con …*	*so·no kwee kon …*
(the UN)	*(l'ONU)*	*(lo·noo)*
my colleagues	*i miei colleghi*	*ee myay ko·le·gee*
(two) others	*(due) altri*	*(doo·e) al·tree*

Here's my business card.
Ecco il mio biglietto da visita.
e·ko eel mee·o bee·lye·to da vee·zee·ta

Let me introduce my colleague.
Vorrei presentare il mio collega. m
vo·ray pre·sen·ta·re eel mee·o ko·le·ga
Vorrei presentare la mia collega. f
vo·ray pre·sen·ta·re la mee·a ko·le·ga

I'm alone.
Sono solo/a. m/f
so·no so·lo/a

I'm here for (two) days/weeks.
Sono qui per (due) giorni/ settimane.
so·no kwee per (doo·e) jor·nee/ se·tee·ma·ne

I'm staying at …, room …
Alloggio al …, camera …
a·lo·jo al …, ka·me·ra …

59

Business needs

I have an appointment with ...
Ho un appuntamento con ...   o oo·na·poon·ta·*men*·to kon ...

I need an interpreter.
Ho bisogno di un interprete.   o bee·*zo*·nyo dee oo·neen·*ter*·pre·te

I'm expecting a ...	*Aspetto ...*	a·*spet*·o ...
call	*una telefonata*	*oo*·na te·le·fo·*na*·ta
fax	*un fax*	oon faks

I need ...	*Ho bisogno di ...*	o bee·*zon*·yo dee ...
to use a	*usare un*	oo·*sa*·re oon
computer	*computer*	kom·*pyoo*·ter
to send an	*mandare un*	man·*da*·re oon
email/fax	*email/fax*	e·*mayl*/faks

Is there a/an ...?	*C'è ...?*	che ...
data projector	*un proiettore*	oon pro·ye·*to*·re
laser pointer	*una penna ottica*	*oo*·na *pe*·na o·*tee*·ka
overhead	*una lavagna*	*oo*·na la·*va*·nya
projector	*luminosa*	loo·mee·*no*·sa

After the deal

That went very well.
È andato bene.   e an·*da*·to *be*·ne

Shall we go for a drink/meal?
Andiamo a bere/   an·*dya*·mo a *be*·re/
mangiare qualcosa?   man·*ja*·re kwal·*ko*·za

It's on me.
Offro io.   o·fro ee·o

For additional terms, see **SERVICES**, page 42.

WORK

HELP
Emergencies

Help!	*Aiuto!*	ai·*yoo*·to
Stop!	*Fermi!*	*fer*·mee
Go away!	*Vai via!*	vai *vee*·a
Thief!	*Ladro!*	*la*·dro
Fire!	*Al fuoco!*	al *fwo*·ko
Watch out!	*Attenzione!*	a·ten·*tsyo*·ne

Call ...	*Chiami ...*	*kya*·mee ...
an ambulance	*un'ambulanza*	o·nam·boo·*lan*·tsa
a doctor	*un medico*	oon *me*·dee·ko
the fire	*i vigili del*	ee *vee*·jee·lee del
brigade	*fuoco*	*fwo*·ko
the police	*la polizia*	la po·lee·*tsee*·a

It's an emergency!
  È un'emergenza!   e oo·ne·mer·*jen*·tsa

Could you help me, please?
  Mi può aiutare, per favore?   mee pwo ai·yoo·*ta*·re per fa·*vo*·re

I have to use the telephone.
  Devo fare una telefonata.   *de*·vo fa·re *oo*·na te·le·fo·*na*·ta

I'm lost.
  Mi sono perso/a. m/f   mee *so*·no *per*·so/a

Where are the toilets?
  Dove sono i gabinetti?   *do*·ve *so*·no ee ga·bee·*ne*·tee

Leave me alone!
  Lasciami in pace!   *la*·sha·mee een *pa*·che

Police

Where's the police station?
Dov'è il posto di polizia?   do·*ve* eel *pos*·to dee po·lee·*tsee*·a

I want to report an offence.
Voglio fare una denuncia.   *vo*·lyo *fa*·re *oo*·na de·*noon*·cha

I've been raped.
Sono stato/a violentato/a. m/f   *so*·no *sta*·to/a vyo·len·*ta*·to/a

I've been assaulted.
Sono stato aggredito/a. m/f   *so*·no *sta*·to/a a·gre·*dee*·to/a

I've been robbed.
Sono stato/a derubato/a. m/f   *so*·no *sta*·to/a de·roo·*ba*·to/a

I've lost my ... My ... was/were stolen.	*Ho perso ...* *Mi hanno* *rubato ...*	o *per*·so ... mee *a*·no roo·*ba*·to ...
backpack	*il mio zaino*	eel *mee*·o *dzai*·no
bags	*i miei* *bagagli*	ee mee·*ay* ba·*ga*·lyee
credit card	*la mia carta* *di credito*	la *mee*·a *kar*·ta dee *kre*·dee·to
handbag	*la mia borsa*	la *mee*·a *bor*·sa
jewellery	*i miei gioielli*	ee mee·*ay* jo·ye·le·lee
money	*i miei soldi*	ee mee·*ay* sol·dee
passport	*il mio* *passaporte*	eel *mee*·o pa·sa·*por*·te
travellers cheques	*i miei* *assegni di* *viaggio*	ee mee·*ay* a·*se*·nyee dee vee·*a*·jo
wallet	*portafoglio*	por·ta·*fo*·lyo

I want to	Vorrei	vo·*ray*
contact my ...	contattare ...	kon·ta·*ta*·re ...
embassy	*la mia ambasciata*	la *mee*·a am·ba·*sha*·ta
consulate	*il mio consolato*	eel *mee*·o kon·so·*la*·to

I have insurance.
Ho l'assicurazione.   o la·see·koo·ra·*tsyo*·ne

Can I have a receipt for my insurance?
Può darmi una ricevuta per   pwo *dar*·mee *oo*·na ree·che·*voo*·ta per
la mia assicurazione?   la *mee*·a a·see·koo·ra·*tsyo*·ne

I have a prescription for this drug.
Ho una ricetta per questa   o *oo*·na re·*che*·ta per *kwe*·sta
medicina.   me·dee·*chee*·na

Health

Where's the	Dov'è ... più	do·*ve* ... pyoo
nearest ...?	vicino/a? m/f	vee·*chee*·no/a
(night) chemist	*la farmacia* f	la far·ma·*chee*·a
	(di turno)	(dee *toor*·no)
dentist	*il/la dentista* m/f	eel/la den·*tee*·sta
doctor	*il medico* m	eel *me*·dee·ko
hospital	*l'ospedale* m	los·pe·*da*·le
medical centre	*l'ambulatorio* m	lam·boo·la·*to*·ryo
optometrist	*l'ottico* m	*lo*·tee·ko

I need a doctor (who speaks English).
Ho bisogno di un medico   o bee·*zo*·nyo dee oon *me*·dee·ko
(che parli inglese).   (ke *par*·lee een·*gle*·ze)

Could I see a female doctor?
Posso vedere una dottoressa?   *po*·so ve·*de*·re *oo*·na do·to·*re*·sa

Can the doctor come here?
Può venire qui il medico?   pwo ve·*nee*·re kwee eel *me*·dee·ko

I've run out of my medication.
Ho finito la mia   o fee·*nee*·to la *mee*·a
medicina.   me·dee·*chee*·na

I've been	*Sono stato/a*	*so*·no *sta*·to/a
vaccinated for ...	*vaccinato/a per ...* m/f	va·chee·*na*·to/a per ...
hepatitis A/B/C	*l'epatite A/B/C*	le·pa·*tee*·te a/bee/chee
tetanus	*il tetano*	eel *te*·ta·no
typhoid	*il tifo*	eel *tee*·fo

I need ...	*Ho bisogno di ...*	o bee·*zo*·nyo dee ...
new glasses	*nuovi occhiali*	*nwo*·vee o·*kya*·lee
contact	*nuove lenti a*	*nwo*·ve *len*·tee a
lenses	*contatto*	kon·*ta*·to

Symptoms, conditions & allergies

HELP

I'm sick.
Mi sento male.   mee *sen*·to *ma*·le

I've been injured.
Sono stato/a ferito/a. m/f   *so*·no *sta*·to/a fe·*ree*·to/a

It hurts here.
Mi fa male qui.   mee fa *ma*·le kwee

I've been vomiting.
Ho vomitato alcune volte.   o vo·mee·*ta*·to al·*koo*·ne *vol*·te

I can't sleep.
Non riesco a dormire.   non *ryes*·ko a dor·*mee*·re

I feel ...	Mi sento ...	mee *sen*·to ...
better	meglio	*me*·lyo
strange	strano/a m/f	*stra*·no/a
weak	debole	*de*·bo·le
worse	peggio	*pe*·jo

I feel ...	Sono ...	*so*·no ...
anxious	ansioso/a m/f	an·*syo*·zo/a
depressed	depresso/a m/f	de·*pre*·so/a

I feel ...	Ho ...	o ...
dizzy	il capogiro	eel ka·po·*gee*·ro
hot and	vampate di	vam·*pa*·te dee
cold	calore	ka·*lo*·re
nauseous	la nausea	la *now*·ze·a
shivery	i brividi	ee *bree*·vee·dee

I have a/ an ...	Ho ...	o ...
allergy	un'allergia	oo·na·ler·*jee*·a
cold	un raffreddore	oon ra·fre·*do*·re
cough	la tosse	la *to*·se
diarrhoea	la diarrea	la dee·a·*re*·a
fever	la febbre	la *fe*·bre
headache	mal di testa	mal dee *tes*·ta
heart	un problema	oon pro·*ble*·ma
condition	cardiaco	kar·*dya*·ko
migraine	un'emicrania	oo·ne·mee·*kran*·ya
swelling	un gonfiore	oon gon·*fyo*·re
sore throat	mal di gola	mal dee *go*·la

I'm ...	Sono ...	*so*·no ...
asthmatic	asmatico/a m/f	az·*ma*·tee·ko/a
diabetic	diabetico/a m/f	dee·a·*be*·tee·ko/a
epileptic	epilettico/a m/f	e·pee·le·tee·ko/a

HELP

65

I've (recently) had ...
 Ho avuto ...   o a·*voo*·to ...
 (di recente).   (dee re·*chen*·te)

I'm on medication for ...
 Prendo la   *pren*·do la
 medicina per ...   me·dee·*chee*·na per ...

I need something for ...
 Ho bisogno di   o bee·*zo*·nyo dee
 qualcosa per ...   kwal·*ko*·za per ...

Do I need a prescription for ...?
 C'è bisogno di una   che bee·*zo*·nyo dee *oo*·na
 ricetta per ...?   re·*che*·ta per ...

How many times a day?
 Quante volte al giorno?   *kwan*·te *vol*·te al *jor*·no

I'm allergic to ...   *Sono*   *so*·no
     allergico/a ... m/f   a·*ler*·jee·ko/a ...

antibiotics	*agli anti-*	*a*·lyee an·tee·
	biotici	bee·*o*·tee·chee
anti-	*agli*	*a*·lyee
inflammatories	*antinfiammatori*	an·teen·fya·ma·*to*·ree
aspirin	*all'aspirina*	a·las·pee·*ree*·na
bees	*alle api*	*a*·le *a*·pee
codeine	*alla codeina*	*a*·la ko·de·*ee*·na
penicillin	*alla*	*a*·la
	penicillina	pe·nee·chee·*lee*·na
pollen	*al polline*	al po·*lee*·ne

I have a skin allergy.
 Ho un'allergia alla pelle.   o oo·na·ler·*jee*·a *a*·la *pe*·le

For food-related allergies, see **EAT & DRINK** page 34.

HELP

66

Numbers

0	*zero*	dze·ro		18	*diciotto*	dee·cho·to
1	*uno*	oo·no		19	*diciannove*	dee·cha·no·ve
2	*due*	doo·e		20	*venti*	ven·tee
3	*tre*	tre		21	*ventuno*	ven·too·no
4	*quattro*	kwa·tro		22	*ventidue*	ven·tee·doo·e
5	*cinque*	cheen·kwe		30	*trenta*	tren·ta
6	*sei*	say		40	*quaranta*	kwa·ran·ta
7	*sette*	se·te		50	*cinquanta*	cheen·kwan·ta
8	*otto*	o·to		60	*sessanta*	se·san·ta
9	*nove*	no·ve		70	*settanta*	se·tan·ta
10	*dieci*	dye·chee		80	*ottanta*	o·tan·ta
11	*undici*	oon·dee·chee		90	*novanta*	no·van·ta
12	*dodici*	do·dee·chee		91	*novantuno*	no·van·too·no
13	*tredici*	tre·dee·chee		100	*cento*	chen·to
14	*quattordici*	kwa·tor·dee·chee		200	*duecento*	doo·e·chen·to
15	*quindici*	kween·dee·chee		300	*trecento*	tre·chen·to
16	*sedici*	se·dee·chee		1,000	*mille*	mee·le
17	*diciassette*	dee·cha·se·te		2,000	*duemila*	doo·e·mee·la

Colours

dark ...

   ... *scuro/a* m/f   skoo·ro/a

black	*nero/a* m/f	ne·ro/a
blue	*azzurro/a* m/f	a·dzoo·ro/a
brown	*marrone*	ma·ro·ne
green	*verde*	ver·de
orange	*arancione*	a·ran·chyo·ne

light ...

   ... *chiaro/a* m/f   kya·ro/a

pink	*rosa*	ro·za
purple	*viola*	vyo·la
red	*rosso/a* m/f	ro·so/a
yellow	*giallo/a* m/f	ja·lo/a
white	*bianco/a* m/f	byan·ko/a

Time & Dates

What time is it?	*Che ora è?*	ke *o*·ra e
It's one o'clock.	*È l'una.*	e *loo*·na
It's (two) o'clock.	*Sono le (due).*	so·no le (*doo*·e)
Five past (one).	*(L'una) e cinque.*	(*loo*·na) e *cheen*·kwe
Quarter past (one).	*(L'una) e un quarto.*	(*loo*·na) e oon *kwar*·to
Half past (one).	*(L'una) e mezza.*	(*loo*·na) e me·dza
Quarter to (eight).	*(Le otto) meno un quarto.*	(le *o*·to) me·no oon *kwar*·to
Twenty to (eight).	*(Le otto) meno venti.*	(le *o*·to) me·no ven·tee
At what time ...?	*A che ora ...?*	a ke *o*·ra ...
At ...	*Alle ...*	*a*·le ...

Monday	*lunedì*	loo·ne·*dee*
Tuesday	*martedì*	mar·te·*dee*
Wednesday	*mercoledì*	mer·ko·le·*dee*
Thursday	*giovedì*	jo·ve·*dee*
Friday	*venerdì*	ve·ner·*dee*
Saturday	*sabato*	*sa*·ba·to
Sunday	*domenica*	do·*me*·nee·ka

January	*gennaio*	je·*na*·yo
February	*febbraio*	fe·*bra*·yo
March	*marzo*	*mar*·tso
April	*aprile*	a·*pree*·le
May	*maggio*	*ma*·jo
June	*giugno*	*joo*·nyo
July	*luglio*	*loo*·lyo
August	*agosto*	a·*gos*·to
September	*settembre*	se·*tem*·bre
October	*ottobre*	o·*to*·bre
November	*novembre*	no·*vem*·bre
December	*dicembre*	dee·*chem*·bre

spring	primavera	pree·ma·ve·ra
summer	estate	es·ta·te
autumn	autunno	ow·too·no
winter	inverno	een·ver·no

What date is it today?
Che giorno è oggi?   ke *jor*·no e *o*·jee

It's (15 December).
È (il quindici)   e (eel *kween*·dee·chee
dicembre).   dee·*chem*·bre)

last ...

night	*ieri notte*	*ye*·ree *no*·te
week	*la settimana*	la se·tee·*ma*·na
	scorsa	*skor*·sa
month	*il mese scorso*	eel *me*·ze *skor*·so
year	*l'anno scorso*	*la*·no *skor*·so

next ...

week	*la settimana*	la se·tee·*ma*·na
	prossima	*pro*·see·ma
month	*il mese prossimo*	eel *me*·ze *pro*·see·mo
year	*l'anno prossimo*	*la*·no *pro*·see·mo

since (May)   *da (maggio)*   da (*ma*·jo)

tomorrow ...   *domani ...*   do·*ma*·nee ...

morning	*mattina*	ma·*tee*·na
afternoon	*pomeriggio*	po·me·*ree*·jo
evening	*sera*	*se*·ra

yesterday ...   *ieri ...*   *ye*·ree ...

morning	*mattina*	ma·*tee*·na
afternoon	*pomeriggio*	po·me·*ree*·jo
evening	*sera*	*se*·ra

A

aboard *a bordo* a bor·do
accident *incidente* m een·chee·*den*·te
accommodation *alloggio* m a·*lo*·jo
adaptor *spina* f *multipla* spee·na
   mool·tee·pla
address *indirizzo* m een·dee·*ree*·tso
admission price *prezzo* m *d'ingresso*
   pre·tso deen·*gre*·so
after *dopo* do·po
afternoon *pomeriggio* m po·me·*ree*·jo
aftershave *dopobarba* m do·po·*bar*·ba
again *di nuovo* dee *nwo*·vo
air-conditioned *ad aria condizionata* ad
   a·rya kon·dee·*tsyo*·na·ta
airline *linea* f *aerea* lee·ne·a a·*e*·re·a
airport *aeroporto* m a·e·ro·*por*·to
airport tax *tassa* f *aeroportuale* ta·sa
   a·e·ro·por·*twa*·le
aisle (plane, train) *corridoio* m
   ko·ree·*do*·yo
alarm clock *sveglia* f *sve*·lya
alcohol *alcol* m *al*·kol
all (plural) *tutti/e* m/f *too*·tee/*too*·te
all (singular) *tutto/a* m/f *too*·to/a
allergy *allergia* f a·ler·*jee*·a
ambulance *ambulanza* f am·boo·*lan*·tsa
and *e* e
ankle *caviglia* f ka·*vee*·lya
antibiotics *antibiotici* m pl
   an·tee·bee·o·tee·chee
antique *pezzo* m *di antiquariato* pe·tso dee
   an·tee·kwa·*rya*·to
antiseptic *antisettico* m an·tee·se·tee·ko
appointment *appuntamento* m
   a·poon·ta·*men*·to
archaeological *archeologico/a* m/f
   ar·ke·o·*lo*·jee·ko/a

architect *architetto* m ar·kee·*te*·to
architecture *architettura* f ar·kee·te·*too*·ra
arm *braccio* m *bra*·cho
arrivals *arrivi* m pl a·*ree*·vee
art *arte* f *ar*·te
art gallery *galleria* f *d'arte* ga·le·*ree*·a
   dar·te
artist *artista* m&f ar·*tee*·sta
ashtray *portacenere* m por·ta·*che*·ne·re
at *a* a
aunt *zia* f *tsee*·a
Australia *Australia* f ow·*stra*·lya
automatic teller machine (ATM)
   Bancomat m *ban*·ko·mat
awful *orrendo/a* m/f o·ren·do/a

B

B&W (film) *in bianco e nero* een *byan*·ko
   e *ne*·ro
baby *bimbo/a* m/f *beem*·bo/a
baby food *cibo* m *da bebè* chee·bo da be·*be*
back (body) *schiena* f *skye*·na
backpack *zaino* m *dzai*·no
bad *cattivo/a* m/f ka·tee·vo/a
bag (general) *borsa* f *bor*·sa
bag (shopping) *sacchetto* m sa·*ke*·to
baggage *bagaglio* m ba·*ga*·lyo
baggage allowance *bagaglio* m *consentito*
   ba·*ga*·lyo kon·sen·*tee*·to
baggage claim *ritiro* m *dei bagagli* ree·*tee*·ro
   ba·*ga*·lyee
bakery *panetteria* f pa·ne·te·*ree*·a
band (music) *gruppo* m *groo*·po
bandage *fascia* f *fa*·sha
Band-aids *cerotti* m pl che·*ro*·tee
bank (money) *banca* f *ban*·ka
bank account *conto* m *in banca* con·to
   een *ban*·ka

banknote *banconota* f ban·ko·*no*·ta

bar *locale* m lo·*ka*·le

bath *bagno* m *ba*·nyo

bathroom *bagno* m *ba*·nyo

battery *pila* f *pee*·la

beach *spiaggia* f *spya*·ja

beautiful *bello/a* m/f *be*·lo/a

beauty salon *parrucchiere* m pa·roo·*kye*·re

because *perché* per·*ke*

bed *letto* m *le*·to

bedroom *camera* f *da letto* *ka*·me·ra da *le*·to

beer *birra* f *bee*·ra

before *prima* *pree*·ma

behind *dietro* dye·tro

best *migliore* mee·*lyo*·re

better *migliore* mee·*lyo*·re

bicycle *bicicletta* f bee·chee·*kle*·ta

big *grande* *gran*·de

bill (account) *conto* m *kon*·to

birthday *compleanno* m kom·ple·*a*·no

black *nero/a* m/f *ne*·ro/a

blanket *coperta* f ko·*per*·ta

blister *vescica* f ve·*shee*·ka

blocked *bloccato/a* m/f blo·*ka*·to/a

blood *sangue* m *san*·gwe

blood group *gruppo* m *sanguigno* *groo*·po san·*gwee*·nyo

blue (dark) *blu* bloo

blue (light) *azzurro/a* m/f a·*dzoo*·ro/a

board (a plane, ship) *salire su* sa·*lee*·re su

boarding house *pensione* f pen·*syo*·ne

boarding pass *carta* f *d'imbarco* *kar*·ta *deem*·bar·ko

boat *barca* f *bar*·ka

book *libro* m *lee*·bro

book (make a booking) *prenotare* pre·no·*ta*·re

booked out *completo/a* m/f kom·*ple*·to/a

bookshop *libreria* f lee·bre·*ree*·a

boots *stivali* m pl stee·*va*·lee

border *confine* m kon·*fee*·ne

boring *noioso/a* m/f no·*yo*·zo/a

bottle *bottiglia* f bo·*tee*·lya

bottle opener *apribottiglie* m a·pree·bo·*tee*·lye

bowl *piatto* m *fondo* *pya*·to *fon*·do

box *scatola* f *ska*·to·la

boy *bambino* m bam·*bee*·no

boy(friend) *ragazzo* m ra·*ga*·tso

bra *reggiseno* m re·jee·*se*·no

bread *pane* m *pa*·ne

breakfast (prima) *colazione* f (*pree*·ma) ko·la·*tsyo*·ne

bridge *ponte* m *pon*·te

briefcase *valigetta* f va·lee·*je*·ta

broken *rotto/a* m/f *ro*·to/a

broken down *guastato/a* m/f gwas·*ta*·to/a

brother *fratello* m fra·*te*·lo

brown *marrone* m/f *ma*·ro·ne

budget *bilancio* m bee·*lan*·cho

buffet (meal) *pasto* m *freddo* *pas*·to *fre*·do

building *edificio* m e·dee·*fee*·cho

bum *culo* m *koo*·lo

burn *bruciare* broo·*cha*·re

bus (city) *autobus* m *ow*·to·boos

bus (coach) *pullman* m *pool*·man

bus station *stazione* f *d'autobus* sta·*tsyo*·ne *dow*·to·boos

bus stop *fermata* f *d'autobus* fer·*ma*·ta *dow*·to·boos

business *affari* m pl a·*fa*·ree

business class *classe* f *business* *kla*·se *beez*·nes

business person *uomo/donna d'affari* m/f *wo*·mo/*do*·na da·*fa*·ree

business trip *viaggio* m *d'affari* vee·*a*·jo da·*fa*·ree

butcher's shop *macelleria* f ma·che·le·*ree*·a

button *bottone* m bo·*to*·ne

buy *comprare* kom·*pra*·re

C

café *bar* m bar
calculator *calcolatrice* f kal·ko·la·*tree*·che
camera *macchina* f *fotografica* ma·kee·na fo·to·*gra*·fee·ka
camp site *campeggio* m kam·*pe*·jo
can (tin) *scatola* f *ska*·to·la
can opener *apriscatole* m a·pree·*ska*·to·le
Canada *Canada* m *ka*·na·da
cancel *cancellare* kan·che·*la*·re
car *macchina* f *ma*·kee·na
car hire *autonoleggio* m ow·to·no·*le*·jo
car owner's title *libretto* m *di circolazione* lee·*bre*·to dee cheer·ko·la·*tsyo*·ne
car registration *bollo* m *di circolazione* *bo*·lo dee cheer·ko·la·*tsyo*·ne
cash *soldi* m pl *sol*·dee
cash register *cassa* f *ka*·sa
cashier *cassiere/a* m/f ka·sye·re/a
cassette *cassetta* f ka·se·ta
castle *castello* m kas·*te*·lo
cathedral *duomo* m *dwo*·mo
CD *cidì* m chee·*dee*
centimetre *centimetro* m chen·*tee*·me·tro
centre *centro* m *chen*·tro
chair *sedia* f *se*·dya
chairlift (skiing) *seggiovia* f se·jo·*vee*·a
change *cambiare* kam·*bya*·re
change (coins) *spiccioli* m pl spee·cho·lee
change (money) *resto* m *res*·to
change room (sport) *spogliatoio* m spo·*lya*·*to*·yo
cheap *economico/a* m/f e·ko·*no*·mee·ko/a
check *controllare* kon·tro·*la*·re
check (bill) *conto* m *kon*·to
check-in (airport) *accetazione* f a·che·ta·*tsyo*·ne
check-in (hotel) *registrazione* f re·jee·stra·*tsyo*·ne

cheese *formaggio* m for·*ma*·jo
chef *cuoco/a* m/f *kwo*·ko/a
chemist *farmacista* m&f far·ma·*chee*·sta
cheque *assegno* m a·*se*·nyo
chest *petto* m *pe*·to
chicken *pollo* m *po*·lo
child *bambino/a* m/f bam·*bee*·no/a
child seat *seggiolino* m se·jo·*lee*·no
chocolate *cioccolato* m cho·ko·*la*·to
Christmas *Natale* m na·*ta*·le
church *chiesa* f *kye*·za
cigar *sigaro* m *see*·ga·ro
cigarette *sigaretta* f see·ga·*re*·ta
cigarette lighter *accendino* m a·chen·*dee*·no
cinema *cinema* m *chee*·ne·ma
circus *circo* m *cheer*·ko
city *città* f chee·*ta*
classical *classico/a* m/f *kla*·see·ko/a
clean *pulito/a* m/f poo·*lee*·to/a
cleaning *pulizia* f poo·lee·*tsee*·a
client *cliente* m&f klee·*en*·te
cloakroom *guardaroba* m gwar·da·*ro*·ba
closed *chiuso/a* m/f *kyoo*·zo/a
clothing *abbigliamento* m a·*bee*·lya·men·to
clothing store *negozio* m *di abbigliamento* ne·*go*·tsyo dee a·*bee*·lya·men·to
coat *cappotto* m ka·*po*·to
coffee *caffè* m ka·fè
coins *monete* f pl mo·*ne*·te
cold *freddo/a* m/f *fre*·do/a
colleague *collega* m&f ko·*le*·ga
collect call *chiamata* f *a carico del destinatario* kya·*ma*·ta a *ka*·ree·ko del des·tee·na·*ta*·ryo
colour *colore* m ko·*lo*·re
comb *pettine* m *pe*·tee·ne
comfortable *comodo/a* m/f *ko*·mo·do/a

LOOK UP

commission *commissione* f ko-mee-syo-ne
companion *compagno/a* m/f kom-pa-nyo/a
company (firm) *ditta* f dee-ta
complain *lamentarsi* la-men-tar-see
complimentary (free) *gratuito/a* m/f gra-too-ee-to/a
computer *computer* m kom-pyoo-ter
concert *concerto* m kon-cher-to
conditioner *balsamo* m per i capelli bal-sa-mo per ee ka-pe-lee
condom *preservativo* m pre-zer-va-tee-vo
confirm (a booking) *confermare* kon-fer-ma-re
connection (transport) *coincidenza* f ko-een-chee-den-tsa
constipation *stitichezza* f stee-tee-ke-tsa
consulate *consolato* m kon-so-la-to
contact lenses *lenti* f pl a contatto len-tee a kon-ta-to
convenience store *alimentari* m a-lee-men-ta-ree
cook *cuoco/a* m/f kwo-ko/a
cook *cucinare* koo-chee-na-re
cost *costare* kos-ta-re
cotton balls *batuffoli* m pl di cotone ba-too-fo-lee dee ko-to-ne
cough *tossire* to-see-re
cough medicine *sciroppo* m per la tosse shee-ro-po per la to-se
countryside *campagna* f kam-pa-nya
court (tennis) *campo* m da tennis kam-po da te-nees
cover charge (restaurant) *coperto* m ko-per-to
cover charge (venue) *ingresso* m een-gre-so
craft (product) *pezzo* m d'artigianato pe-tso dar-tee-ja-na-to
craft (trade) *mestiere* m mes-tye-re
cream (food) *panna* f pa-na

credit card *carta* f di credito kar-ta dee kre-dee-to
cup *tazza* f ta-tsa
currency exchange *cambio* m valuta kam-byo va-loo-ta
current (electricity) *corrente* f ko-ren-te
customs *dogana* f do-ga-na
cut *tagliare* ta-lya-re
cutlery *posate* f pl po-za-te

D

dance *ballare* ba-la-re
dancing *ballo* m ba-lo
dangerous *pericoloso/a* m/f pe-ree-ko-lo-zo/a
dark *scuro/a* m/f skoo-ro/a
date (day) *data* f da-ta
date of birth *data* f di nascita da-ta dee na-shee-ta
daughter *figlia* f fee-lya
day *giorno* m jor-no
day after tomorrow *dopodomani* do-po-do-ma-nee
day before yesterday *altro ieri* m al-tro ye-ree
delay *ritardo* m ree-tar-do
delicatessen *salumeria* f sa-loo-me-ree-a
dental floss *filo* m dentario fee-lo den-ta-ree-o
dentist *dentista* m&f den-tee-sta
deodorant *deodorante* m de-o-do-ran-te
depart *partire* par-tee-re
department store *grande magazzino* m gran-de ma-ga-dzee-no
departure *partenza* f par-ten-tsa
dessert *dolce* m dol-che
destination *destinazione* f des-tee-na-tsyo-ne

diabetes *diabete* m dee·a·*be*·te

dial tone *segnale* m (acustico) se·*nya*·le (a·*koos*·tee·ko)

diaper *pannolino* m pa·no·*lee*·no

diarrhoea *diarrea* f dee·a·*re*·a

diary *agenda* f a·*jen*·da

dictionary *vocabolario* m vo·ka·bo·*la*·ryo

different *diverso/a* dee·*ver*·so/a

dining car *carrozza* f *ristorante* ka·ro·*tsa* rees·to·*ran*·te

dinner *cena* f *che*·na

direct *diretto/a* m/f dee·*re*·to/a

direct-dial *telefono* m *diretto* te·*le*·fo·no dee·*re*·to

direction *direzione* f dee·re·*tsyo*·ne

dirty *sporco/a* m/f *spor*·ko/a

disabled *disabile* dee·za·*bee*·le

discount *sconto* m *skon*·to

disk (computer) *dischetto* m dees·*ke*·to

divorced *divorziato/a* m/f dee·vor·*tsya*·to/a

doctor *medico* m *me*·dee·ko

dog *cane* m *ka*·ne

dollar *dollaro* m *do*·la·ro

dope (drugs) *roba* f *ro*·ba

double bed *letto* m *matrimoniale* *le*·to ma·tree·mo·*nya*·le

double room *camera* f *doppia* ka·mer·a *do*·pya

down *giù* joo

dress *abito* m a·*bee*·to

drink *bere* be·re

drive *guidare* gwee·*da*·re

drivers licence *patente* f (di guida) pa·*ten*·te (dee gwee·da)

drunk *ubriaco/a* m/f oo·bree·*a*·ko/a

dry *secco/a* m/f *se*·ko/a

dry *asciugare* a·shoo·ga·re

dummy (pacifier) *ciucciotto* m choo·*cho*·to

E

each *ciascuno/a* m/f chas·*koo*·no/a

ear *orecchio* m o·*re*·kyo

early *presto* m/f *pres*·to

earrings *orecchini* m pl o·re·*kee*·nee

east *est* m est

Easter *Pasqua* f *pas*·kwa

economy class *classe* f *turistica* *kla*·se too·ree·stee·ka

electricity *elettricità* f e·le·tree·chee·*ta*

elevator *ascensore* m a·shen·*so*·re

email *email* m e·*mayl*

embassy *ambasciata* f am·ba·*sha*·ta

emergency *emergenza* f e·mer·*jen*·tsa

empty *vuoto/a* m/f *vwo*·to/a

end *fine* f *fee*·ne

end *finire* fee·*nee*·re

engagement (couple) *fidanzamento* m fee·dan·tsa·*men*·to

engine *motore* m mo·to·re

engineer *ingegnere* m&f een·je·*nye*·re

England *Inghilterra* f een·geel·*te*·ra

English *inglese* een·*gle*·ze

enough *abbastanza* a·bas·*tan*·tsa

enter *entrare* en·*tra*·re

entertainment guide *guida* f *agli spettacoli* *gwee*·da a·lyee spe·*ta*·ko·lee

entry *entrata* f en·*tra*·ta

escalator *scala* f *mobile* ska·la mo·*bee*·le

euro *euro* m e·*oo*·ro

Europe *Europa* f e·oo·ro·pa

evening *sera* f *se*·ra

everything *tutto* m *too*·to

exchange *cambiare* kam·*bya*·re

exchange rate *tasso* m *di cambio* ta·so dee *kam*·byo

exhibition *esposizione* f es·po·zee·*tsyo*·ne

exit *uscita* f oo·*shee*·ta

expensive *caro/a* m/f *ka·*ro/a
express *espresso/a* m/f es·*pre·*so/a
express mail *posta* f *prioritaria* pos·ta
  pree·o·ree·*ta·*rya
eye *occhio* m o·kyo

F

face *faccia* f *fa·*cha
fall (autumn) *autunno* m ow·*too·*no
family *famiglia* f fa·*mee·*lya
family name *cognome* m ko·*nyo·*me
fan (machine) *ventilatore* m
  ven·tee·la·to·re
fan (person) *tifoso/a* m/f tee·fo·zo/a
far *lontano/a* m/f lon·ta·no/a
fashion *moda* f mo·da
fast *veloce* ve·*lo·*che
fat *grasso/a* m/f gra·so/a
father *padre* m pa·dre
father-in-law *suocero* m swo·che·ro
faucet *rubinetto* m roo·bee·*ne·*to
faulty *difettoso/a* m/f dee·fe·*to·*zo/a
fax *fax* m faks
feel *sentire* sen·tee·re
ferry *traghetto* m tra·*ge·*to
fever *febbre* f fe·bre
fiancé(e) *fidanzato/a* m/f fee·dan·*tsa·*to/a
film (cinema) *film* m feelm
film speed *ASA* a·za
fine (payment) *multa* f *mool·*ta
finger *dito* m dee·to
first class *prima classe* f *pree·*ma kla·se
first-aid kit *valigetta* f *del pronto soccorso*
  va·lee·*je·*ta del *pron·*to so·*kor·*so
fish shop *pescheria* f pe·ske·*ree·*a
fishing *pesca* f pe·ska
flash (camera) *flash* m flesh
flashlight (torch) *torcia* f *elettrica* tor·cha
  e·*le·*tree·ka

flight *volo* m vo·lo
floor (storey) *piano* m *pya·*no
florist *fioraio* m&f fyo·*ra·*yo
flu *influenza* f een·floo·*en·*tsa
fly *volare* vo·la·re
food *cibo* m chee·bo
food supplies *provviste* m pl *alimentari*
  pro·*vee·*ste a·lee·men·*ta·*ree
foot *piede* m pye·de
football (soccer) *calcio* m *kal·*cho
footpath *marciapiede* m mar·cha·pye·de
foreign *straniero/a* m/f stra·*nye·*ro/a
forest *foresta* f fo·res·ta
fork *forchetta* f for·*ke·*ta
fortnight *quindici giorni* m pl
  *kween·*dee·chee jor·nee
fragile *fragile* fra·jee·le
France *Francia* f fran·cha
free (gratis) *gratuito/a* m/f gra·*too·*ee·to/a
fresh *fresco/a* m/f fres·ko/a
fridge *frigorifero* m free·go·ree·fe·ro
friend *amico/a* m/f a·*mee·*ko/a
frozen *congelato/a* m/f kon·je·*la·*to/a
fruit *frutta* f froo·ta
fry *friggere* free·je·re
frying pan *padella* f pa·de·la
full *pieno/a* m/f pye·no/a
funny *divertente* dee·ver·*ten·*te
furniture *mobili* m pl mo·bee·lee

G

game (play) *gioco* m jo·ko
game (sport) *partita* f par·*tee·*ta
garden *giardino* m jar·dee·no
gas (for cooking) *gas* m gaz
gas (petrol) *benzina* f ben·dzee·na
gastroenteritis *gastroenterite* f
  gas·tro·en·te·*ree·*te

gay *gay* gei
Germany *Germania* f jer·*ma*·nya
gift *regalo* m re·*ga*·lo
girl(friend) *ragazza* f ra·*ga*·tsa
glasses (spectacles) *occhiali* m pl o·*kya*·lee
gloves *guanti* m pl *gwan*·tee
go *andare* an·*da*·re
gold *oro* m *o*·ro
golf course *campo* m*da golf* kam·po
    da golf
good *buono/a* m/f *bwo*·no/a
grandchild *nipote* m&f nee·*po*·te
grandfather *nonno* m *no*·no
grandmother *nonna* f *no*·na
great *ottimo/a* m/f o·tee·mo/a
green *verde* ver·de
grey *grigio/a* m/f *gree*·jo/a
grocery *drogheria* f dro·ge·*ree*·a
guesthouse *pensione* f pen·*syo*·ne
guide (person) *guida* f *gwee*·da
guidebook *guida* f (*turistica*) gwee·da
    (too·*ree*·stee·ka)
guided tour *visita* f *guidata* vee·zee·ta
    gwee·*da*·ta
gym *palestra* f pa·*le*·stra

H

hairdresser *parrucchiere/a* m/f
    pa·roo·*kye*·re/a
hand *mano* f *ma*·no
handbag *borsetta* f bor·*se*·ta
handicrafts *oggetti* m pl *d'artigianato*
    o·*je*·tee dar·tee·ja·*na*·to
handkerchief *fazzoletto* m fa·tso·*le*·to
handmade *fatto/a* m/f *a mano* fa·to/a
    a *ma*·no
handsome *bello/a* m/f *be*·lo/a
happy *felice* m/f fe·*lee*·che
hard (not soft) *duro/a* m/f *doo*·ro/a

hat *cappello* m ka·*pe*·lo
have *avere* a·*ve*·re
hay fever *febbre* f *da fieno* fe·bre da *fye*·no
he *lui* loo·ee
head *testa* f *tes*·ta
headache *mal* m *di testa* mal dee *tes*·ta
headlights *fari* m pl *fa*·ree
heart *cuore* m *kwo*·re
heart condition *problema* m *cardiaco*
    pro·*ble*·ma kar·*dee*·a·ko
heat *caldo* m *kal*·do
heater *stufa* f *stoo*·fa
heavy *pesante* pe·*zan*·te
help *aiutare* a·yoo·*ta*·re
here *qui* kwee
high *alto/a* m/f *al*·to/a
hike *escursione* f *a piedi* es·koor·*syo*·ne
    a *pye*·de
hiking *escursionismo* m *a piedi*
    es·koor·syo·*neez*·mo a *pye*·de
hire *noleggiare* no·le·*ja*·re
hitchhike *fare l'autostop* fa·re *low*·to·stop
holidays *vacanze* f pl va·*kan*·tse
home *casa* f *ka*·za
homosexual *omosessuale* m&f
    o·mo·se·*swa*·le
honeymoon *luna* f *di miele* loo·na dee
    mye·le
horse riding *andare a cavallo* an·da·re
    a ka·*va*·lo
hospital *ospedale* m os·pe·*da*·le
hot *caldo/a* m/f *kal*·do/a
hotel *albergo* m al·*ber*·go
hour *ora* f *o*·ra
husband *marito* m ma·*ree*·to

I

ice *ghiaccio* m *gya*·cho
ice cream *gelato* m je·*la*·to

identification *documento* m *d'identità* do-koo-*men*-to dee-den-tee-*ta*

identification card (ID) *carta* f *d'identità* *kar*-ta dee-den-tee-*ta*

ill *malato/a* m/f ma-*la*-to/a

important *importante* eem-por-*tan*-te

impossible *impossibile* eem-po-*see*-bee-le

included *compreso/a* m/f kom-*pre*-zo/a

indigestion *indigestione* f een-dee-je-*styo*-ne

infection *infezione* f een-fe-*tsyo*-ne

influenza *influenza* f een-floo-*en*-tsa

information *informazioni* f pl een-for-ma-*tsyo*-nee

injection *iniezione* f ee-nye-*tsyo*-ne

injured *ferito/a* m/f fe-*ree*-to/a

injury *ferita* f fe-*ree*-ta

insurance *assicurazione* f a-see-koo-ra-*tsyo*-ne

intermission *intervallo* m een-ter-*va*-lo

Internet (café) *Internet (point)* m *een*-ter-net (poynt)

interpreter *interprete* m/f een-*ter*-pre-te

Ireland *Irlanda* f eer-*lan*-da

iron (for clothes) *ferro* m *da stiro* fe-ro da *stee*-ro

island *isola* f *ee*-zo-la

IT *informatica* f een-for-*ma*-tee-ka

itch *prurito* m proo-*ree*-to

itinerary *itinerario* m ee-tee-ne-*ra*-ryo

J

jacket *giacca* f *ja*-ka

jeans *jeans* m pl jeens

jet lag *disturbi* m pl *da fuso orario* dees-*toor*-bee da *foo*-zo o-*ra*-ryo

jewellery *gioielli* m pl jo-*ye*-lee

job *lavoro* m la-*vo*-ro

journalist *giornalista* m&f jor-na-*lee*-sta

jumper *maglione* m ma-*lyo*-ne

K

kilogram *chilo* m *kee*-lo

kilometre *chilometro* m kee-*lo*-me-tro

kind *gentile* jen-*tee*-le

kitchen *cucina* f koo-*chee*-na

knee *ginocchio* m jee-*no*-kyo

knife *coltello* m kol-*te*-lo

L

lake *lago* m *la*-go

language *lingua* f *leen*-gwa

laptop (computer) *portatile* m (kom-*pyoo*-ter) por-*ta*-tee-le

last *ultimo/a* m/f *ool*-tee-mo/a

late *in ritardo* een ree-*tar*-do

laundrette *lavanderia* f *a gettone* la-van-de-*ree*-a je-*to*-ne

laundry *lavanderia* f la-van-de-*ree*-a

law *legge* f *le*-je

lawyer *avvocato/a* m/f a-vo-*ka*-to/a

laxatives *lassativi* m pl la-sa-*tee*-vee

leather *cuoio* m *kwo*-yo

left (direction) *sinistra* f see-*nee*-stra

left luggage (office) *deposito* m *bagagli* de-*po*-zee-to ba-*ga*-lyee

leg *gamba* f *gam*-ba

lens *obiettivo* m o-bye-*tee*-vo

lesbian *lesbica* f *lez*-bee-ka

less (di) *meno* (dee) *me*-no

letter *lettera* f *le*-te-ra

library *biblioteca* f bee-blyo-*te*-ka

life jacket *giubbotto* m *di salvataggio* joo-*bo*-to dee sal-va-*ta*-jo

lift (elevator) *ascensore* m a-shen-*so*-re

M English–Italian dictionary

LOOK UP

light *luce* f *loo*-che
light (colour) *chiaro/a* m/f *kya*-ro/a
light (not heavy) *leggero/a* m/f le-*je*-ro/a
light meter *esposimetro* m es-po-*zee*-me-tro
lighter *accendino* m a-chen-*dee*-no
like *piacere* pya-*che*-re
lipstick *rossetto* m ro-*se*-to
liquor store *bottiglieria* f bo-tee-lye-*ree*-a
listen *ascoltare* as-kol-*ta*-re
local *locale* lo-*ka*-le
locked *chiuso/a* m/f *(a chiave)* kyoo-zo/a (a *kya*-ve)
long *lungo/a* m/f *loon*-go/a
lost *perso/a* m/f *per*-so/a
loud *forte* m/f *for*-te
love *amare* a-*ma*-re
lubricant *lubrificante* m loo-bree-fee-*kan*-te
luggage *bagaglio* m ba-*ga*-lyo
luggage lockers *armadietti* m pl *per i bagagli* ar-ma-*dye*-tee per ee ba-*ga*-lyee
lunch *pranzo* m *pran*-dzo

M

mail *posta* f *pos*-ta
mail box *buca* f *delle lettere boo*-ka de-le *le*-te-re
make-up *trucco* m *troo*-ko
man *uomo* m *wo*-mo
manager *manager* m *me*-nee-je
map *pianta* f *pyan*-ta
market *mercato* m mer-*ka*-to
married *sposato/a* m/f spo-*za*-to/a
massage *massaggio* m ma-*sa*-jo
match (sport) *partita* f par-*tee*-ta
matches *fiammiferi* m pl fya-*mee*-fe-ree
meat *carne* f *kar*-ne

medicine *medicina* f me-dee-*chee*-na
menu *menu* m me-*noo*
message *messaggio* m me-*sa*-jo
metro station *stazione* f *della metropolitana* sta-*tsyo*-ne de-la me-tro-po-lee-*ta*-na
microwave oven *forno* m *a microonde for*-no a mee-kro-on-de
midnight *mezzanotte* f me-dza *no*-te
milk *latte* m *la*-te
millimetre *millimetro* m mee-*lee*-me-tro
mineral water *acqua* f *minerale* a-kwa mee-ne-*ra*-le
minute *minuto* m mee-*noo*-to
mirror *specchio* m *spe*-kyo
mobile phone (telefono) *cellulare* m (te-*le*-fo-no) che-loo-*la*-re
modem *modem* m *mo*-dem
modern *moderno/a* m/f mo-*der*-no/a
money *denaro* m de-*na*-ro
month *mese* m *me*-ze
more (di) *più* (dee) *pyoo*
morning *mattina* f ma-*tee*-na
mother *madre* f *ma*-dre
mother-in-law *suocera* f *swo*-che-ra
motorway (tollway) *autostrada* f ow-to-*stra*-da
mountain *montagna* f mon-*ta*-nya
mouth *bocca* f *bo*-ka
movie *film* m feelm
museum *museo* m moo-*ze*-o
music *musica* f *moo*-zee-ka

N

nail clippers *tagliaunghie* m ta-lya-*oon*-gye
name *nome* m *no*-me
napkin *tovagliolo* m to-va-*lyo*-lo
nappy *pannolino* m pa-no-*lee*-no

78

near (to) *vicino (a)* vee-*chee*-no (a)
nearby *vicino/a* m/f vee-*chee*-no/a
needle (sewing) *ago* m a-go
needle (syringe) *ago* m *da siringa* a-go da
  see-*reen*-ga
Netherlands *Paesi Bassi* m pl pa-e-zee
  ba-see
new *nuovo/a* m/f nwo-vo/a
New Year's Day *Capodanno* m *ka*-po da-no
New Year's Eve *san Silvestro* m san
  seel-*ves*-tro
New Zealand *Nuova Zelanda* f nwo-va
  dze-*lan*-da
news *notizie* f pl no-*tee*-tsye
newsagency *edicola* f e-*dee*-ko-la
newspaper *giornale* m jor-*na*-le
next *prossimo/a* m/f *pro*-see-mo/a
night *notte* f *no*-te
no *no* no
noisy *rumoroso/a* m/f roo-mo-ro-zo/a
nonsmoking *non fumatore* non
  foo-ma-*to*-re
north *nord* m nord
notebook *quaderno* m kwa-*der*-no
nothing *niente* nyen-te
now *adesso* a-*de*-so
number *numero* m *noo*-me-ro
nurse *infermiere/a* m/f een-fer-*mye*-re/a

O

ocean *oceano* m o-*che*-a-no
oil *olio* m o-lyo
on *su* soo
one-way (ticket) *(un biglietto di) solo*
  andata (oon bee-*lye*-to dee) so-lo an-*da*-ta
only *solo* so-lo
open *aperto/a* m/f a-*per*-to/a
open *aprire* a-*pree*-re

opening hours *orario* m *di apertura*
  o-*ra*-ryo dee a-per-*too*-ra
orange (colour) *arancione* a-ran-*cho*-ne
other *altro/a* m/f *al*-tro/a
outside *fuori* fwo-ree

P

pacifier *ciuccotto* m choo-*cho*-to
packet (general) *pacchetto* m pa-*ke*-to
padlock *lucchetto* m loo-*ke*-to
pain *dolore* m do-*lo*-re
painful *doloroso/a* m/f do-lo-ro-zo/a
painkillers *analgesico* m an-al-*je*-zee-ko
painter *pittore/pittrice* m/f pee-*to*-re/
  pee-*tree*-che
painting (the art) *pittura* f pee-*too*-ra
palace *palazzo* m pa-*la*-tso
pants *pantaloni* m pl pan-ta-*lo*-nee
panty liners *salva slip* m pl *sal*-va sleep
pantyhose *collant* f pl ko-*lant*
paper *carta* f *kar*-ta
paperwork *moduli* m pl *mo*-doo-lee
parcel *pacchetto* m pa-*ke*-to
parents *genitori* m pl je-nee-*to*-ree
park *parco* m *par*-ko
party (celebration) *festa* f *fes*-ta
passenger *passeggero/a* m/f pa-se-*je*-ro/a
passport *passaporto* m pa-sa-*por*-to
path *sentiero* m sen-*tye*-ro
payment *pagamento* m pa-ga-*men*-to
pen (ballpoint) *penna* f *(a sfera)* pe-na
  (a *sfe*-ra)
pencil *matita* f ma-*tee*-ta
penis *pene* m pe-ne
penknife *temperino* m tem-pe-*ree*-no
pensioner *pensionato/a* m/f
  pen-syo-*na*-to/a
per (day) *al (giorno)* al (*jor*-no)

perfume *profumo* m pro-*foo*-mo
petrol *benzina* f ben-*dzee*-na
petrol station *distributore* m
  dee-stree-boo-*to*-re
pharmacy *farmacia* f far-ma-*chee*-a
phone book *elenco* m *telefonico* e-*len*-ko
  te-le-*fo*-nee-ko
phone box *cabina* f *telefonica* ka-*bee*-na
  te-le-*fo*-nee-ka
phone call *chiamata* f kya-*ma*-ta
photo *foto* f *fo*-to
photographer *fotografo* m fo-*to*-gra-fo
photography *fotografia* f fo-to-gra-*fee*-a
phrasebook *vocabolarietto* m
  vo-ka-bo-la-*rye*-to
picnic *picnic* m *peek*-neek
pill *pillola* f pee-*lo*-la
pillow *cuscino* m koo-*shee*-no
pillowcase *federa* f *fe*-de-ra
pink *rosa* m/f *ro*-za
plane *aereo* m a-*e*-re-o
plate *piatto* m *pya*-to
platform *binario* m bee-*na*-ryo
play (theatre) *commedia* f ko-*me*-dya
plug (bath) *tappo* m *ta*-po
plug (electricity) *spina* f *spee*-na
point *indicare* een-dee-*ka*-re
police (civilian) *polizia* f po-lee-*tsee*-a
police (military) *carabinieri* m pl
  ka-ra-bee-*nye*-ree
police station *posto* m di *polizia* *pos*-to dee
  po-lee-*tsee*-a
pool (swimming) *piscina* f pee-*shee*-na
post code *codice* m *postale* ko-dee-che
  pos-*ta*-le
post office *ufficio* m *postale* oo-*fee*-cho
  pos-*ta*-le
postcard *cartolina* f kar-to-*lee*-na
pound (money) *sterlina* f ster-*lee*-na
pregnant *incinta* een-*cheen*-ta

prescription *ricetta* f ree-*che*-ta
present (gift) *regalo* m re-*ga*-lo
price *prezzo* m *pre*-tso
printer (computer) *stampante* f
  stam-*pan*-te
private *privato/a* m/f pree-*va*-to/a
pub *pub* m poob
public telephone *telefono* m *pubblico*
  te-*le*-fo-no poo-*blee*-ko
purple *viola* vee-*o*-la

Q

quiet *tranquillo/a* m/f tran-*kwee*-lo/a

R

rain *pioggia* m *pyo*-ja
raincoat *impermeabile* m
  eem-per-me-*a*-bee-le
rare *raro/a* m/f *ra*-ro/a
razor *rasoio* m (*elettrico*) ra-*zo*-yo
  (e-*le*-tree-ko)
razor blades *lamette* f pl (*da barba*)
  la-*me*-te (da *bar*-ba)
receipt *ricevuta* f ree-che-*voo*-ta
recommend *raccomandare*
  ra-ko-man-*da*-re
red *rosso/a* m/f *ro*-so/a
refrigerator *frigo* m *free*-go
refund *rimborso* m reem-*bor*-so
registered mail (*posta*) *raccomandata* f
  (*pos*-ta) ra-ko-man-*da*-ta
remote control *telecomando* m
  te-le-ko-*man*-do
repair *riparare* ree-pa-*ra*-re
reservation *prenotazione* f
  pre-no-ta-*tsyo*-ne
restaurant *ristorante* m rees-to-*ran*-te

return (ticket) *(biglietto)* di andata e ritorno (bee-*lye*-to) dee an-*da*-ta e ree-*tor*-no

right (direction) *a destra* a de-*stra*

river *fiume* m *fyoo*-me

rock (music) *(musica)* rock (moo-zee-ka) rok

romantic *romantico/a* m/f ro-man-*tee*-ko/a

room *camera* f *ka*-me-ra

ruins *rovine* f pl ro-*vee*-ne

S

safe *sicuro/a* m/f see-*koo*-ro/a

safe sex *rapporti* m pl *protetti* ra-*por*-tee pro-*te*-tee

sanitary napkins *assorbenti* m pl *igienici* as-or-*ben*-tee ee-*je*-nee-chee

scarf *sciarpa* f *shar*-pa

science *scienza* f *shen*-tsa

scissors *forbici* f pl *for*-bee-chee

Scotland *Scozia* f *sko*-tsya

sculpture *scultura* f skool-*too*-ra

sea *mare* m *ma*-re

season *stagione* f sta-*jo*-ne

seat (place) *posto* m *pos*-to

seatbelt *cintura* f *di sicurezza* cheen-*too*-ra dee see-koo-*re*-tsa

second class *seconda classe* f se-*kon*-da *kla*-se

self-service *self-service* self-*ser*-vees

service *servizio* m ser-*vee*-tsyo

service charge *servizio* m ser-*vee*-tsyo

service station *stazione* f *di servizio* sta-*tsyo*-ne dee ser-*vee*-tsyo

sex *sesso* m *se*-so

shade *ombra* f *om*-bra

shape *forma* f *for*-ma

share (with) *condividere* kon-dee-*vee*-de-re

shave *fare la barba* fa-re la *bar*-ba

shaving cream *crema* f *da barba* kre-ma da *bar*-ba

sheet (bed) *lenzuolo* m len-*tswo*-lo

shirt *camicia* f ka-*mee*-cha

shoe shop *negozio* m *di scarpe* ne-*go*-tsyo dee *skar*-pe

shoes *scarpe* f pl *skar*-pe

shop *negozio* m ne-*go*-tsyo

shopping centre *centro* m *commerciale* *chen*-tro ko-mer-*cha*-le

short (height) *basso/a* m/f *ba*-so/a

short (length) *corto/a* m/f *kor*-to/a

shorts *pantaloncini* m pl pan-ta-lon-*chee*-nee

shoulder *spalla* f *spa*-la

show *mostrare* mos-*tra*-re

shower *doccia* f *do*-cha

shut *chiuso/a* m/f kyoo-zo/a

sick *malato/a* m/f ma-*la*-to/a

silk *seta* f *se*-ta

silver *argento* m ar-*jen*-to

single (man) *celibe* m *che*-lee-be

single (woman) *nubile* f *noo*-bee-le

single room *camera* f *singola* ka-me-ra *seen*-go-la

sister *sorella* f so-*re*-la

size (general) *dimensioni* f pl dee-men-*syo*-nee

skiing *sci* m shee

skirt *gonna* f *go*-na

sleep *dormire* dor-*mee*-re

sleeping bag *sacco* m *a pelo* sa-ko a *pe*-lo

sleeping car *vagone* m *letto* va-*go*-ne *le*-to

slice *fetta* f *fe*-ta

slide (film) *diapositiva* m dee-a-po-zee-*tee*-va

slowly *lentamente* len-ta-*men*-te

small *piccolo/a* m/f pee-ko-lo/a

smell *odore* m o-*do*-re

smoke *fumare* foo-*ma*-re

snack *spuntino* m spoon·*tee*·no

snow *neve* f *ne*·ve

soap *sapone* m sa·*po*·ne

socks *calzini* m pl cal·*tsee*·nee

some *alcuni/e* m/f pl al·*koo*·nee/al·*koo*·ne

son *figlio* m *fee*·lyo

soon *fra poco* fra *po*·ko

south *sud* m sood

souvenir *ricordino* m ree·kor·*dee*·no

souvenir shop *negozio* m *di souvenir* ne·*go*·tsyo dee *soo*·ve·neer

Spain *Spagna* f *spa*·nya

speak *parlare* par·*la*·re

speed limit *limite* m *di velocità* lee·mee·te dee ve·lo·chee·*ta*

spoon *cucchiaio* m koo·*kya*·yo

sports store *negozio* m *di articoli sportivi* ne·*go*·tsyo dee ar·*tee*·ko·lee spor·*tee*·vee

sprain *storta* f *stor*·ta

spring (season) *primavera* f pree·ma·*ve*·ra

square (town) *piazza* f *pya*·tsa

stairway *scale* f pl *ska*·le

stamp *francobollo* m fran·ko·*bo*·lo

standby (ticket) (in lista) *d'attesa* (een *lee*·sta) da·*te*·za

station *stazione* f sta·*tsyo*·ne

stationer *cartolaio* m kar·to·*la*·yo

stockings *calze* f pl *kal*·tse

stolen *rubato/a* m/f roo·*ba*·to/a

stomach *stomaco* m *sto*·ma·ko

stomachache *mal* m *di pancia* mal dee *pan*·cha

stop *fermare* fer·*ma*·re

student *studente/studentessa* m/f stoo·*den*·te/stoo·den·*te*·sa

subway *metropolitana* f me·tro·po·lee·*ta*·na

suitcase *valigia* f va·*lee*·ja

summer *estate* f es·*ta*·te

sun *sole* m *so*·le

sunblock *crema* f *solare* *kre*·ma so·*la*·re

sunburn *scottatura* f sko·ta·*too*·ra

sunglasses *occhiali* m pl *da sole* o·*kya*·lee da *so*·le

sunscreen *crema* f *solare* *kre*·ma so·*la*·re

sunset *tramonto* m tra·*mon*·to

supermarket *supermercato* m soo·per·mer·*ka*·to

surface mail *posta* f *ordinaria* pos·ta or·dee·*na*·rya

surname *cognome* m ko·*nyo*·me

sweater *maglione* m ma·*lyo*·ne

sweet *dolce* *dol*·che

swim *nuotare* nwo·*ta*·re

swimming pool *piscina* f pee·*shee*·na

swimsuit *costume* m *da bagno* ko·*stoo*·me da *ba*·nyo

T

tailor *sarto* m *sar*·to

take (photo) *fare* *fa*·re

tampons *tamponi* m pl tam·*po*·nee

tanning lotion *lozione* f *abbronzante* lo·*tsyo*·ne a·bron·*dzan*·te

tap (faucet) *rubinetto* m roo·bee·*ne*·to

tasty *gustoso/a* m/f goo·*sto*·zo/a

taxi *tassì* m ta·*see*

taxi stand *posteggio* m *di tassì* po·*ste*·jo dee ta·*see*

tea *tè* m te

teaspoon *cucchiaino* m koo·kya·*ee*·no

telegram *telegramma* m te·le·*gra*·ma

telephone *telefono* m te·*le*·fo·no

telephone *telefonare* te·le·fo·*na*·re

television *televisione* f te·le·vee·*zyo*·ne

tennis *tennis* m *te*·nees

tennis court *campo* m *da tennis kam*·po da *te*·nees
theatre *teatro* m te·a·tro
there *là* la
this (one) *questo* m/f *kwe*·sto/a
throat *gola* f *go*·la
ticket *biglietto* m bee·*lye*·to
ticket machine *distributore* m *automatico di biglietti* dee·stree·boo·*to*·re ow·to·ma·tee·ko dee bee·*lye*·tee
ticket office *biglietteria* f bee·lye·te·*ree*·a
time difference *differenza* f *di fuso orario* dee·fe·*ren*·tsa dee foo·zo o·ra·ryo
timetable *orario* m o·ra·ryo
tin (can) *scatoletta* f ska·to·*le*·ta
tin opener *apriscatole* f a·pree·*ska*·to·le
tip (gratuity) *mancia* f *man*·cha
tired *stanco/a* m/f *stan*·ko/a
tissues *fazzolettini* m pl *di carta* fa·tso·le·*tee*·nee dee *kar*·ta
toast *pane* m *tostato* pa·ne tos·ta·to
toaster *tostapane* m tos·ta·*pa*·ne
today *oggi* o·jee
together *insieme* een·*sye*·me
toilet *gabinetto* m ga·bee·*ne*·to
toilet paper *carta* f *igienica* kar·ta ee·je·nee·ka
tomorrow *domani* do·*ma*·nee
tonight *stasera* sta·se·ra
too (expensive) *troppo (caro/a)* tro·po (*ka*·ro/a)
toothache *mal* m *di denti* mal dee *den*·tee
toothbrush *spazzolino* m *da denti* spa·tso·*lee*·no da den·tee
toothpaste *dentifricio* m den·tee·*free*·cho
torch (flashlight) *torcia* f *elettrica* tor·cha e·*le*·tree·ka
tour *gita* f *jee*·ta
tourist *turista* m&f too·*ree*·sta
tourist office *ufficio* m *del turismo* oo·*fee*·cho del too·*reez*·mo

towel *asciugamano* m a·shoo·ga·*ma*·no
train *treno* m tre·no
train station *stazione* f *(ferroviaria)* sta·*tsyo*·ne (fe·ro·vyar·ya)
transit lounge *sala* f *di transito* sa·la dee *tran*·zee·to
translate *tradurre* tra·*doo*·re
travel agency *agenzia* f *di viaggio* a·jen·*tsee*·a dee vee·a·jo
travel sickness (air) *mal* m *di aereo* mal dee a·e·re·o
travel sickness (car) *mal* m *di macchina* mal dee ma·kee·na
travel sickness (sea) *mal* m *di mare* mal dee ma·re
travellers cheque *assegno* m *di viaggio* a·*se*·nyo dee vee·a·jo
trolley (luggage) *carrello* m ka·re·lo
trousers *pantaloni* m pl pan·ta·*lo*·nee
try *provare* pro·va·re
T-shirt *maglietta* f ma·*lye*·ta
TV *TV* f tee·*voo*
tweezers *pinzette* f pl peen·*tse*·te
twin beds *due letti* doo·e le·tee
twins *gemelli/e* m/f pl je·me·lee/je·me·le
tyre *gomma* f *go*·ma

U

umbrella *ombrello* m om·*bre*·lo
uncomfortable *scomodo/a* m/f *sko*·mo·do/a
underwear *biancheria* f *intima* byan·ke·*ree*·a een·tee·ma
university *università* f oo·nee·ver·see·*ta*
until *fino a* fee·no a
up *su* soo
urgent *urgente* m/f oor·*jen*·te
USA *Stati* m pl *Uniti d'America* sta·tee oo·*nee*·tee da·me·ree·ka

LOOK UP

V

vacant *libero/a* m/f lee·be·ro/a
vacation *vacanza* f va·kan·tsa
vaccination *vaccinazione* f
va·chee·na·tsyo·ne
vagina *vagina* f va·jee·na
validate *convalidare* kon·va·lee·da·re
valuable *prezioso/a* m/f pre·tsyo·zo/a
vegetable *verdura* f ver·doo·ra
vegetarian *vegetariano/a* m/f
ve·je·ta·rya·no/a
video camera *videocamera* f
vee·de·o·ka·me·ra
video tape *videonastro* m
vee·de·o·nas·tro
view *vista* f vee·sta
visa *visto* m vee·sto

W

wait *aspettare* as·pe·ta·re
waiter *cameriere/a* m/f ka·mer·ye·re/a
waiting room *sala d'attesa*
sa·la da·te·sa
wake up *svegliarsi* sve·lyar·see
walk *passeggiata* f pa·se·ja·ta
walk *camminare* ka·mee·na·re
warm *tiepido/a* m/f tye·pee·do/a
wash (something) *lavare* la·va·re
washing machine *lavatrice* f la·va·tree·che
watch *guardare* gwar·da·re
water *acqua* f a·kwa
water bottle *borraccia* f bo·ra·cha
week *settimana* f se·tee·ma·na
weekend *fine* m *settimana* fee·ne
se·tee·ma·na
west *ovest* m o·vest

wheelchair *sedia* f *a rotelle* se·dya a
ro·te·le
when *quando* kwan·do
where *dove* do·ve
white *bianco/a* m/f byan·ko/a
who *chi* kee
why *perché* per·ke
wife *moglie* f mo·lye
window (car, plane) *finestrino* m
fee·nes·tree·no
window (general) *finestra* f
fee·nes·tra
wine *vino* m vee·no
wine cellar *cantina* f kan·tee·na
wine tasting *degustazione* f *dei vini*
de·goos·ta·tsyo·ne day vee·nee
winery *cantina* f kan·tee·na
winter *inverno* m een·ver·no
without *senza* sen·tsa
woman *donna* f do·na
wool *lana* f la·na
write *scrivere* skree·ve·re

Y

year *anno* m a·no
yellow *giallo/a* m/f ja·lo/a
yes *sì* see
yesterday *ieri* ye·ree
you (inf) *tu* too
you (polite) *Lei* lay
youth hostel *ostello* m *della gioventù*
os·te·lo de·la jo·ven·too

Z

zoo *giardino* m *zoologico* jar·dee·no
dzo·o·lo·jee·ko

A

abbastanza a·bas·*tan*·tsa *enough*
abbigliamento m a·bee·lya·*men*·to *clothing*
abito m a·*bee*·to *dress*
accetazione f a·che·ta·*tsyo*·ne *check-in (airport)*
acqua f a·kwa *water*
acqua f **minerale** ak·wa mee·ne·*ra*·le *mineral water*
adesso a·*de*·so *now*
aeroporto m a·e·ro·*por*·to *airport*
affari m pl a·*fa*·ree *business*
agenzia f **di viaggio** a·jen·*tsee*·a dee vee·*a*·jo *travel agency*
aiutare a·yoo·*ta*·re *help*
albergo m al·*ber*·go *hotel*
alloggio m a·*lo*·jo *accommodation*
altro ieri m ye·*ree* *day before yesterday*
ambasciata f am·ba·*sha*·ta *embassy*
amico/a m/f a·*mee*·ko/a *friend*
anno m *a*·no *year*
aperto/a m/f a·*per*·to/a *open*
appuntamento m a·poon·ta·*men*·to *appointment • date*
arancia f a·*ran*·cha *orange (fruit)*
arancione a·ran·*cho*·ne *orange (colour)*
aria f **condizionata** *a*·ree·a kon·dee·*tsyo*·na·ta *air conditioning*
armadietti m pl **per i bagagli** ar·ma·*dye*·tee per ee ba·*ga*·lyee *luggage lockers*
arrivi m pl a·*ree*·vee *arrivals*
assegno m **di viaggio** a·*se*·nyo dee vee·*a*·jo *travellers cheque*
assicurazione f a·see·koo·ra·*tsyo*·ne *insurance*
autobus m *ow*·to·boos *bus (city)*
autonoleggio m ow·to·no·*le*·jo *car hire*
azzurro/a m/f a·*dzoo*·ro/a *(light) blue*

B

bagaglio in eccedenza ba·*ga*·lyo een e·che·*den*·tsa *excess bagagge*
bagaglio m ba·*ga*·lyo *luggage*
bagaglio m **consentito** ba·*ga*·lyo kon·sen·*tee*·to *baggage allowance*
bagno m *ba*·nyo *bath • bathroom*
bambino/a m/f bam·*bee*·no/a *child*
Bancomat m *ban*·ko·mat *automatic teller machine (ATM)*
barca f *bar*·ka *boat*
bebé m&f be·*be* *baby*
bello/a m/f *be*·lo/a *beautiful • handsome • good (weather)*
bere *be*·re *drink*
bevanda f be·*van*·da *drink*
biancheria f **intima** byan·ke·*ree*·a *een*·tee·ma *underwear*
bianco e nero byan·ko e *ne*·ro *B&W*
bianco/a m/f *byan*·ko/a *white*
bicicletta f bee·chee·*kle*·ta *bicycle*
biglietteria f bee·lye·te·ree·a *ticket office*
biglietto m bee·*lye*·to *ticket*
biglietto m **di andata e ritorno** bee·*lye*·to dee an·*da*·ta e ree·*tor*·no *return ticket*
bimbo/a m/f *beem*·bo/a *baby*
binario m bee·*na*·ryo *platform*
birra f *bee*·ra *beer*
blu bloo *blue (dark)*
bollo m **di circolazione** *bo*·lo dee cheer·ko·la·*tsyo*·ne *car registration*
borsa f *bor*·sa *bag (general)*
bottiglia f bo·*tee*·lya *bottle*

C

cabina f **telefonica** ka·*bee*·na te·le·*fo*·nee·ka *phone box*
caffè m ka·*fe* *coffee*

caldo/a m/f *kal*·do/a *hot*
calzini m pl kal·*tsee*·nee *socks*
cambiare kam·*bya*·re *change*
cambio m *kam*·byo *exchange • change*
cambio m **valuta** *kam*·byo va·*loo*·ta *currency exchange*
camera **doppia** *ka*·me·ra *do*·pya *double room*
camera f **da letto** *ka*·me·ra da *le*·to *bedroom*
camera f **singola** *ka*·me·ra *seen*·go·la *single room*
camicia f ka·*mee*·cha *shirt*
camminare ka·mee·*na*·re *walk*
campagna f kam·*pa*·nya *countryside*
cancellare kan·che·*la*·re *cancel*
cane m *ka*·ne *dog*
cappello m ka·*pe*·lo *hat*
cappotto m ka·*po*·to *coat*
carabinieri m pl ka·ra·bee·*nye*·ree *police (military)*
carne f *kar*·ne *meat*
caro/a m/f *ka*·ro/a *expensive*
carrozza f **ristorante** ka·*ro*·tsa rees·to·*ran*·te *dining car*
carta f *kar*·ta *paper*
carta f **d'identità** *kar*·ta dee·den·tee·*ta* *identification card (ID)*
carta f **d'imbarco** *kar*·ta deem·*bar*·ko *boarding pass*
carta f **di credito** *kar*·ta dee *kre*·dee·to *credit card*
cartolaio m kar·to·*la*·yo *stationer*
cartolina f kar·to·*lee*·na *postcard*
cassiere/a m/f ka·*sye*·re/a *cashier*
cattivo/a m/f ka·*tee*·vo/a *bad*
celibe m *che*·lee·be *single (man)*
cellulare m che·loo·*la*·re *mobile phone*
cena f *che*·na *dinner*
centro m **commerciale** *chen*·tro ko·mer·*cha*·le *shopping centre*
cerotti m pl che·*ro*·tee *Band-aids*

chi kee *who*
chiave f *kya*·ve *key*
chiuso/a m/f *kyoo*·zo/a *closed • shut • locked*
ciascuno/a m/f chas·*koo*·no/a *each*
cintura f **di sicurezza** cheen·*too*·ra dee see·koo·*re*·tsa *seatbelt*
circo m *cheer*·ko *circus*
città f chee·*ta* *city*
classe f **business** *kla*·se *beez*·nes *business class*
classe f **turistica** *kla*·se too·ree·*stee*·ka *economy class*
collant f pl ko·*lant* *pantyhose*
commedia f ko·*me*·dya *play (theatre)*
comodo/a m/f ko·mo·do/a *comfortable*
compagno/a m/f kom·*pa*·nyo/a *companion • partner (intimate)*
compleanno m kom·ple·*a*·no *birthday*
completo/a m/f kom·*ple*·to/a *booked out*
comprare kom·*pra*·re *buy*
compreso/a m/f kom·*pre*·zo/a *included*
computer m kom·*pyoo*·ter *computer*
condividere kon·dee·vee·*de*·re *share (with)*
confermare kon·fer·*ma*·re *confirm (a booking)*
confine m kon·*fee*·ne *border*
congelato/a m/f kon·je·*la*·to/a *frozen*
conto m *kon*·to *bill (account)*
conto m **in banca** *kon*·to een *ban*·ka *bank account*
convalidare kon·va·lee·*da*·re *validate*
coperta f ko·*per*·ta *blanket*
coperto m ko·*per*·to *cover charge (restaurant)*
cucina f koo·*chee*·na *kitchen*
cucinare koo·chee·*na*·re *cook*
cuoco/a m/f *kwo*·ko/a *cook • chef (restaurant)*
cuoio m *kwo*·yo *leather*
cuscino m koo·*shee*·no *pillow*

D

data f **di nascita** *da*-ta dee *na*-shee-ta *date of birth*

deposito m de-*po*-zee-to *deposit (bank)*

deposito m **bagagli** de-*po*-zee-to ba-*ga*-lyee *left luggage (office)*

diapositiva m dee-a-po-zee-*tee*-va *slide (film)*

dimensioni f pl dee-men-*syo*-nee *size (general)*

diretto/a m/f dee-*re*-to/a *direct*

distributore m **automatico di biglietti** dees-tree-boo-*to*-re ow-to-*ma*-tee-ko dee bee-*lye*-tee *ticket machine*

distributore m **di servizio** dees-tree-boo-*to*-re dee ser-*vee*-tsyo *petrol station • service station*

dito m *dee*-to *finger*

doccia f *do*-cha *shower*

dogana f do-*ga*-na *customs*

domani do-*ma*-nee *tomorrow*

domani mattina do-*ma*-nee ma-*tee*-na *tomorrow morning*

domani pomeriggio do-*ma*-nee po-me-*ree*-jo *tomorrow afternoon*

domani sera do-*ma*-nee se-*ra tomorrow evening*

dopodomani do-po-do-*ma*-nee *day after tomorrow*

dormire dor-*mee*-re *sleep*

dove *do*-ve *where*

drogheria f dro-ge-*ree*-a *grocery*

E

edicola f e-*dee*-ko-la *newsagency*

edificio m e-dee-*fee*-cho *building*

elenco m **telefonico** e-*len*-ko te-le-*fo*-nee-ko *phone book*

entrare en-*tra*-re *enter*

entrata f en-*tra*-ta *entry*

erba f *er*-ba *grass • pot (dope)*

esposizione f es-po-zee-*tsyo*-ne *exhibition*

espresso/a m/f es-*pre*-so/a *express*

est m est *east*

estate f es-*ta*-te *summer*

F

fagioli m pl fa-*jo*-lee *beans*

famiglia f fa-*mee*-lya *family*

fantastico/a m/f fan-*tas*-tee-ko/a *great*

farmacia f far-ma-*chee*-a *pharmacy*

federa f *fe*-de-ra *pillowcase*

figlia f *fee*-lya *daughter*

figlio m *fee*-lyo *son*

finestra f fee-*nes*-tra *window (general)*

finestrino m fee-nes-*tree*-no *window (car, plane)*

foresta f fo-*res*-ta *forest*

fra poco fra *po*-ko *soon*

francobollo m fran-ko-*bo*-lo *stamp*

fratello m fra-*te*-lo *brother*

freno m *fre*-no *brake*

fresco/a m/f *fres*-ko/a *fresh*

fumare foo-*ma*-re *smoke*

G

galleria f **d'arte** ga-le-*ree*-a *dar*-te *art gallery*

gas m gaz *gas (for cooking)*

gentile jen-*tee*-le *kind • nice (person)*

giacca f *ja*-ka *jacket*

giallo/a m/f *ja*-lo/a *yellow*

giardino m jar-*dee*-no *garden*

gioielli m pl jo-*ye*-lee *jewellery*

giornale m jor-*na*-le *newspaper*

giorno m *jor*-no *day*

I Italian–English dictionary

gita f *jee*·ta *tour • trip*
gonna f *go*·na *skirt*
grande *gran*·de *big • large*
grande magazzino m *gran*·de
  ma·ga·*dzee*·no *department store*
gratuito/a m/f gra·*too*·ee·to/a *free
  (gratis) • com pl imentary (free)*
grigio/a m/f *gree*·jo/a *grey*
gruppo sanguigno *groo*·po
  san·*gwee*·nyo *blood group*
guanti m *gwan*·tee *gloves*
guardaroba m gwar·da·*ro*·ba *cloakroom*

I

ieri *ye*·ree *yesterday*
in fondo een *fon*·do *at the bottom •
  after all*
in lista d'attesa een *lee*·stada·*te*·za
  standby (ticket)
in ritardo (adv) een ree·*tar*·do *late*
incidente m een·chee·*den*·te *accident*
influenza f een·floo·*en*·tsa flu • *influenza*
informazioni f pl een·for·ma·*tsyo*·nee
  information
inglese een·*gle*·ze *English*
insieme een·*sye*·me *together*
Internet (point) m een·ter·net (poynt)
  Internet (cafe)
interprete m/f een·*ter*·pre·te *interpreter*
intervallo m een·ter·*va*·lo *intermission*
inverno m een·*ver*·no *winter*
itinerario m ee·tee·ne·*ra*·ryo *itinerary •
  route*

J

jeans m pl jeens *jeans*

L

lana f *la*·na *wool*
latte m *la*·te *milk*
lavanderia la·van·de·*ree*·a *laundry (room)*
lavanderia a gettone la·van·de·*ree*·a a
  je·*to*·ne *laundrette*
lavare la·*va*·re *wash (something)*
lavarsi la·*var*·see *wash (oneself)*
lavatrice f la·va·*tree*·che *washing machine*
Lei pol lay *you (polite)*
lettera f *le*·te·ra *letter*
letto m *le*·to *bed*
letto m **matrimoniale** *le*·to
  ma·tree·mo·*nya*·le *double bed*
libreria f lee·bre·*ree*·a *bookshop*
libretto m **di circolazione** lee·*bre*·to dee
  cheer·ko·la·*tsyo*·ne *car owner's title*
libro m *lee*·bro *book*
linea f **aerea** *lee*·ne·a a·e·*re*·a *airline*
Loro pl pol *lo*·ro *you*
luna f **di miele** *loo*·na dee *mye*·le
  honeymoon

M

macchina f *ma*·kee·na *car • machine*
macchina f **fotografica** *ma*·kee·na
  fo·to·*gra*·fee·ka *camera*
macelleria f ma·che·le·*ree*·a *butcher's shop*
madre f *ma*·dre *mother*
maglione m ma·*lyo*·ne *jumper • sweater*
mancia f *man*·cha *tip (gratuity)*
mangiare man·*ja*·re *eat*
marciapiede m mar·cha·*pye*·de *footpath*
mare m *ma*·re *sea*
marrone m/f ma·*ro*·ne *brown*
mattina f ma·*tee*·na *morning*
medicina f me·dee·*chee*·na *medicine*
medico m *me*·dee·ko *doctor*

menù m me·*noo* menu
mercato m mer·*ka*·to market
mese m *me*·ze month
mezzanotte f me·dza·*no*·te midnight
mezzo m *me*·dzo half
moda f *mo*·da fashion
modem m *mo*·dem modem
moglie f *mo*·lye wife
montagna f mon·*ta*·nya mountain
mostrare mos·*tra*·re show
multa f *mool*·ta fine (payment)
musica f *moo*·zee·ka music

N

Natale m na·*ta*·le Christmas
negozio m ne·*go*·tsyo shop
nero/a m/f *ne*·ro/a black
neve f *ne*·ve snow
no no no
noleggiare no·le·*ja*·re hire
nome m *no*·me name
non non no · not
non fumatore non foo·ma·*to*·re
    nonsmoking
nord m nord north
notte f *no*·te night
nubile f *noo*·bee·le single (woman)
numero m *noo*·me·ro number
numero m di camera *noo*·me·ro dee
    ka·me·ra room number
nuotare nwo·*ta*·re swim

O

occhiali m pl o·*kya*·lee glasses (spectacles)
oggi o·*jee* today
olio m o·*lyo* oil
ora f o·*ra* hour
orario m o·*ra*·ryo timetable
orario m di apertura o·*ra*·ryo dee
    a·per·*too*·ra opening hours

oro m o·ro gold
ospedale m os·pe·*da*·le hospital
ostello m della gioventù os·*te*·lo *de*·la
    jo·ven·*too* youth hostel
ovest m o·vest west

P

padre m *pa*·dre father
pagamento m pa·ga·*men*·to payment
palazzo m pa·*la*·tso palace
pane m *pa*·ne bread
panetteria f pa·ne·te·*ree*·a bakery
pannolino m pa·no·*lee*·no diaper · nappy
pantaloni m pl pan·ta·*lo*·nee pants · trousers
parrucchiere m pa·roo·*kye*·re beauty salon
partenza f par·*ten*·tsa departure
partire par·*tee*·re depart · leave
passaporto m pa·sa·*por*·to passport
passeggero/a m/f pa·se·*je*·ro/a passenger
passeggiata f pa·se·*ja*·ta walk
pasticceria f pa·stee·che·*ree*·a cake shop
pasto m *pas*·to meal
patente f (di guida) pa·*ten*·te
    (deeg*wee*·da) drivers licence
pellicola f pe·*lee*·ko·la film (for camera)
penna f (a sfera) *pe*·na (a *sfe*·ra) pen
    (ballpoint)
pensionato/a m/f pen·syo·*na*·to/a
    pensioner · retired
perché per·*ke* why · because
perso/a m/f *per*·so/a lost
pescheria f pe·ske·*ree*·a fish shop
pezzo m di antiquariato *pe*·tso dee
    an·tee·kwa·*rya*·to antique
piano m *pya*·no floor (storey)
picnic m *peek*·neek picnic
pila f *pee*·la battery
piscina f pe·*shee*·na swimming pool
pittore/pittrice m/f pee·*to*·re/
    pee·*tree*·che painter
pittura f pee·*too*·ra painting (the art)

polizia f po·lee·*tsee*·a police (civilian)
pomeriggio m po·me·*ree*·jo afternoon
portacenere m por·ta·*che*·ne·re ashtray
portatile m por·ta·tee·le laptop
posta f *pos*·ta mail
posta f **ordinaria** *pos*·ta or·dee·*na*·rya surface mail
posta f **prioritaria** *pos*·ta pree·o·ree·*ta*·rya express mail
posteggio m **di tassì** po·*ste*·jo dee ta·*see* taxi stand
posto m **di polizia** *pos*·to dee po·lee·*tsee*·a police station
pranzo m *pran*·dzo lunch
prenotare pre·no·*ta*·re book (make a booking)
preservativo m pre·zer·va·*tee*·vo condom
presto m/f *pres*·to early
prezzo m *pre*·tso price
prima classe f *pree*·ma *kla*·se first class
prima colazione f *pree*·ma ko·la·*tsyo*·ne breakfast
primavera f *pree*·ma·*ve*·ra spring (season)
prossimo/a m/f *pro*·see·mo/a next
pulce f *pool*·che flea
pulito/a m/f *poo·lee*·to/a clean
pulizia f poo·lee·*tsee*·a cleaning
pullman m *pool*·man bus (coach)

Q

quadro m *kwa*·dro painting (canvas)
quando *kwan*·do when
qui kwee here

R

raccomandata f ra·ko·man·*da*·ta registered mail
ragazza f ra·*ga*·tsa girl(friend)
ragazzo m ra·*ga*·tso boy(friend)
regalo m re·*ga*·lo present (gift)

reggiseno m re·jee·se·no bra
registrazione f re·jee·stra·*tsyo*·ne check-in (hotel)
resto m *res*·to change (money)
ricetta f ree·*che*·ta prescription
ricevuta f ree·che·*voo*·ta receipt
rimborso m reem·*bor*·so refund
riparare ree·pa·*ra*·re repair
ritardo m ree·*tar*·do delay
ritiro m **bagagli** ree·*tee*·ro ba·*ga*·lyee baggage claim
ritorno m ree·*tor*·no return
rosa m/f *ro*·za pink
rosso/a m/f *ro*·so/a red
rotto/a m/f *ro*·to/a broken
rubato/a m/f roo·*ba*·to/a stolen

S

sacchetto m sa·*ke*·to bag (shopping)
sacco a pelo *sa*·ko a *pe*·lo sleeping bag
sala di transito *sa*·la dee *tran*·zee·to transit lounge
sala f **d'attesa** *sa*·la da·*te*·za waiting room
salumeria f sa·loo·me·*ree*·a delicatessen
salva slip m pl *sal*·va·sleep panty liners
sarto/a m/f *sar*·to/a tailor
scale f pl *ska*·le stairway
scarpe f pl *skar*·pe shoes
scatola f *ska*·to·la box • carton • can • tin
scheda f **telefonica** *ske*·da te·le·*fo*·nee·ka phone card
schiena f *skye*·na back (body)
sconto m *skon*·to discount
secco/a m/f *se*·ko/a dry
sedile m se·*dee*·le seat (chair)
seggiovia f se·jo·*vee*·a chairlift (skiing)
sentiero m sen·*tye*·ro path • track • trail
senza *sen*·tsa without
servizio m ser·*vee*·tsyo service • service-charge
settimana f se·tee·*ma*·na week

sicuro/a m/f see-*koo*-ro/a *safe*
sigaretta f see-ga-*re*-ta *cigarette*
soccorso m so-*kor*-so *help • aid*
soldi m pl *sol*-dee *money • cash*
solo andata f *so*-lo an-*da*-ta *one-way*
sorella f so-*re*-la *sister*
spiaggia f *spya*-ja *beach*
sporco/a m/f *spor*-ko/a *dirty*
spuntino m spoon-*tee*-no *snack*
stagione f sta-*jo*-ne *season*
stanza f *stan*-tsa *room*
stazione della metropolitana sta-*tsyo*-ne de-la me-tro-po-lee-*ta*-na *metro station*
stazione f d'autobus sta-*tsyo*-ne *dow*-to-boos *bus station*
stazione f ferroviaria sta-*tsyo*-ne fe-ro-*vyar*-ya *train station*
sterlina f ster-*lee*-na *pound (money)*
straniero/a m/f stra-*nye*-ro/a *foreign*
studente/studentessa m/f stoo-*den*-te/ stoo-den-*te*-sa *student*
sud m sood *south*
suocera f *swo*-che-ra *mother-in-law*
supermercato m soo-per-mer-*ka*-to *supermarket*
sveglia f *sve*-lya *alarm clock*

T

tardi *tar*-dee *late*
temperino m tem-pe-*ree*-no *penknife*
tossire to-*see*-re *cough*
traghetto m tra-*ge*-to *ferry*
trucco m *troo*-ko *make-up*
tu too *you (inf)*
tutto m *too*-to *everything*

U

ubriaco/a m/f oo-bree-*a*-ko/a *drunk*
ufficio m oo-*fee*-cho *office*

ufficio m del turismo oo-*fee*-cho del too-*reez*-mo *tourist office*
ufficio m oggetti smarriti o-*je*-tee sma-*ree*-tee *lost property office*
ufficio m postale oo-*fee*-cho pos-*ta*-le *post office*
ultimo/a m/f *ool*-tee-mo/a *last*
uomo m *wo*-mo *man*
uscire con oo-*shee*-re kon *go out with • date*
uscita f oo-*shee*-ta *exit*

V

vacanze f pl va-*kan*-tse *holidays*
vagone m letto va-*go*-ne *le*-to *sleeping car*
valigetta f va-lee-*je*-ta *briefcase*
veloce ve-*lo*-che *fast*
verde *ver*-de *green*
verdura f ver-*doo*-ra *vegetable*
via f aerea *vee*-a a-e-re-a *airmail*
viaggio m d'affari *vya*-jo da-*fa*-ree *business trip*
videoregistratore m vee-de-o-re-jee-str a-*to*-re *video*
vino m *vee*-no *wine*
viola vee-*o*-la *purple*
visita f guidata vee-*see*-ta gwee-*da*-ta *guided tour*
vista f *vee*-sta *view*
vocabolarietto m vo-ka-bo-la-*rye*-to *phrasebook*
vocabolario m vo-ka-bo-*la*-ryo *dictionary*
volo m *vo*-lo *flight*

Z

zaino m *dzai*-no *backpack • knapsack*
zia f *tsee*-a *aunt*

INDEX

INDEX

93

INDEX

don't just stand there, say something!

What kind of traveller are you?

A. You're eating chicken for dinner *again* because it's the only word you know.

B. When no one understands what you say, you step closer and shout louder.

C. When the barman doesn't understand your order, you point frantically at the beer.

D. You're surrounded by locals, swapping jokes, email addresses and experiences – other travellers want to borrow your phrasebook or audio guide.

If you answered A, B, or C, you NEED Lonely Planet's language products ...

- **Lonely Planet Phrasebooks** – for every phrase you need in every language you want
- **Lonely Planet Fast Talk** – essential language for short trips and weekends away
- **Lonely Planet Real Talk** – downloadable language audio guides from www.lonelyplanet.com to your MP3 player

... and this is why

- **Talk to everyone everywhere**
  Over 120 languages, more than any other publisher
- **The right words at the right time**
  Quick-reference colour sections, two-way dictionary, easy pronunciation, every possible subject - and audio to support it

Lonely Planet Offices

Australia	**USA**	**UK**
90 Maribyrnong St, Footscray, Victoria 3011	150 Linden St, Oakland, CA 94607	72-82 Rosebery Ave, London EC1R 4RW
☎ 03 8379 8000	☎ 510 893 8555	☎ 020 7841 9000
fax 03 8379 8111	fax 510 893 8572	fax 020 7841 9001
✉ talk2us@lonelyplanet.com.au	✉ info@lonelyplanet.com	✉ go@lonelyplanet.co.uk

www.lonelyplanet.com